EMPLOYMENT LAW

Visit the *Law Express Series* Companion Website at
www.pearsoned.co.uk/lawexpress to find valuable **student**
learning material including:

- A Study Plan test to assess how well you know the subject
  before you begin your revision
- Interactive quizzes to test your knowledge of the main points
  from each chapter of the book
- Further examination questions and guidelines for answering
  them
- Interactive flashcards to help you revise the main terms and
  cases
- Printable versions of the topic maps and checklists

LawExpress

Understand quickly. Revise effectively.
Take exams with confidence.

EMPLOYMENT LAW

David Cabrelli
Lecturer in Law and Solicitor
University of Edinburgh

PEARSON
Longman

Harlow, England • London • New York • Boston • San Francisco • Toronto • Sydney • Singapore • Hong Kong
Tokyo • Seoul • Taipei • New Delhi • Cape Town • Madrid • Mexico City • Amsterdam • Munich • Paris • Milan

Pearson Education Limited
Edinburgh Gate
Harlow
Essex CM20 2JE
England

and Associated Companies throughout the world

Visit us on the World Wide Web at:
www.pearsoned.co.uk

First published 2008

ISBN: 978-1-4058-5952-3

British Library Cataloguing-in-Publication Data
A catalogue record for this book is available from the British Library

10 9 8 7 6 5 4 3 2 1
11 10 09 08 07

Typeset by 3 in 10pt Helvetica Condensed
Printed in Great Britain by Henry Ling Ltd., at the Dorset Press, Dorchester, Dorset

The publisher's policy is to use paper manufactured from sustainable forests.

Contents

Supporting resources
Visit **www.pearsoned.co.uk/lawexpress** to find valuable online resources

Companion Website for students
▪ A Study Plan test to assess how well you know the subject before you begin your revision
▪ Interactive quizzes to test your knowledge of the main points from each chapter of the book
▪ Further examination questions and guidelines for answering them
▪ Interactive flashcards to help you revise the main terms and cases
▪ Printable versions of the topic maps and checklists

Also: The regularly maintained Companion Website provides the following features:

▪ Search tool to help locate specific items of content
▪ E-mail results and profile tools to send results of quizzes to instructors
▪ Online help and support to assist with website usage and troubleshooting

For more information please contact your local Pearson Education sales representative or visit **www.pearsoned.co.uk/lawexpress**

Dedication and acknowledgements

I would like to dedicate this book to my mother, Rosanna Cabrelli. Thanks go to Zoë Botterill and Cheryl Cheasley at Pearson for their patience and encouragement. The feedback of the anonymous reviewers of the draft chapters was also most helpful and I would like to thank them. In addition, the University of Dundee and its students offered excellent insights into certain aspects of employment law which are covered in this book.

David Cabrelli
October 2007

■ Publisher's acknowledgements

Our thanks go to all reviewers who contributed to the development of this text, including students who participated in research and focus groups which helped to shape the series format.

We are grateful to the following for permission to reproduce copyright material:

Unnumbered table (p. 97) adapted from *Guide to the Age Discrimination Regulations 2006*, Tottel Publishing (Sprack, J. 2006), reproduced with kind permission of Tottel Publishing Ltd.; Figures 11.1 and 11.2 are reproduced with the permission of the Controller of HMSO and the Queen's Printer for Scotland.

In some instances we have been unable to trace the owners of copyright material, and we would appreciate any information that would enable us to do so.

Introduction

Employment law is an optional subject which students may take as part of a qualifying undergraduate law degree. Although it is an optional subject, it is extremely popular. Students who choose to take employment law find it very interesting and are often engaged by the breadth of coverage of the topics comprised in the subject. This, together with the fact that employment law is a growth area in legal practice and that more and more solicitors specialise in this area of law, means that its popularity and appeal amongst students is likely to be guaranteed for many years to come.

Employment is an integral part of everyday life. It is a prominent feature in the news and media. Indeed, one of the advantages of studying a subject such as employment law is that many students are also (or have been) employees and are able easily to conceptualise and empathise with many of the topics which are covered. For example, most students will have a basic understanding of what is meant by redundancy, dismissal and discrimination. The contrast with concepts such as 'easements' and 'adverse possession' in land law is stark.

Employment law is statute-based and case law based. The most important statutes are the Employment Rights Act 1996 and the Trade Union and Labour Relations (Consolidation) Act 1992. Employment law is an extremely dynamic area of law and changes very quickly. During your studies, there are likely to be a number of key changes in the law.

This revision guide will help you to identify and apply the law. Its objective is to provide frequent reminders of the importance of understanding the legal definitions of key employment law concepts, such as 'redundancy', 'dismissal', 'trade union', 'direct discrimination' and many others. It is written to be used as a supplement to your course materials, lectures and textbooks. As a revision guide, it should do just that – guide you through revision; it should not be used to cut down on the amount of reading (or thinking) that you have to do in order to succeed. Employment law is a vast, complex and dynamic subject – you should realise this from looking at the size of your recommended textbook. It follows that this revision guide could never be expected to cover the subject in the depth and detail required to succeed in exams and it does not set out to do so. Instead, it aims to provide a concise overall picture of the key areas for revision – reminding you of the headline points to enable you to focus your revision and identify the key points that you need to know.

REVISION NOTES

- Do not be misled by the familiarity of the terminology; ensure that you learn each topic afresh and focus on the legal meanings of the words that you encounter.
- Do rely on this book to guide you through the revision process.
- Do not rely on this book to tell you everything that you need to know about employment law – that is the job of your lecturer's recommended textbook.
- Make sure you consult your own syllabus frequently to check which topics are covered and in how much detail.
- Make use of your lecture notes, handouts, textbooks and other materials as you revise as these will ensure that you have sufficient depth of knowledge.
- Take every possible opportunity to practise your essay-writing and problem-solving technique; get as much feedback as you can.
- Be aware that many questions in employment law combine different topics. Selective revision could leave you unable to answer questions which include reference to material that you have excluded from your revision.

Guided tour

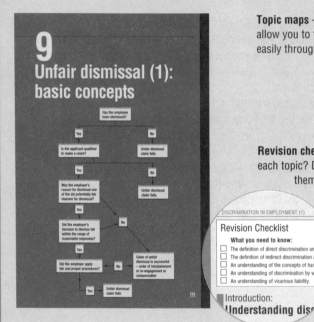

Topic maps – Highlight the main points and allow you to find your way quickly and easily through each chapter.

Revision checklist – How well do you know each topic? Don't panic if you don't know them all, the chapters will help you revise each point so that you will be fully prepared for your exams.

Sample questions – Prepare for what you will be faced with in your exams! Guidance on structuring strong answers is provided at the end of the chapter.

Sample question

Could you answer this question? Below is a typical essay question that could arise on this topic. Guidelines on answering the question are included at the end of the chapter, whilst a sample problem question and guidance on tackling it can be found on the companion website.

Essay question

Analyse how the law distinguishes between persons working under a contract of service and independent contractors. What is the legal significance of this distinction and is the law in need of reform?

Key definition boxes – Make sure you understand essential legal terms.

KEY DEFINITIONS

Fixed-term contract: A contract which endures for a specific period of time and terminates at the end of that period of time.

Repudiatory breach of contract: A breach of a term of a contract which goes to the root of that contract so that on the occurrence of breach the innocent party may be regarded as discharged from further performance of their obligations under the contract.

Problem area boxes – Highlight areas where students most often trip up in exams. Use them to make sure you do not make the same mistakes.

Problem area Which statutory procedure?

Whether an employer requires to follow the statutory standard dismissal and disciplinary procedure in chapter 1 of Part 1 of Sch. 2 to the Employment Act 2002 or the statutory modified dismissal and disciplinary procedure contained in chapter 2 of Part 1 of Sch. 2 to the Employment Act 2002 is determined by reg. 3 of the Employment Act 2002 (Dispute Resolution) Regulations 2004. This provides that the modified procedure is only to be used where the employer has already ~~employee without notice or any payment in lieu of notice. Meanwhile,~~ ~~dure applies where the employer is contemplating dismissal.~~

KEY CASE

Lumley v. *Gye* [1853] 2 ~~gdure~~

Concerning: inducement to

Facts

Miss Wagner had a three-mont~~h~~ which was a rival theatre of the Wagner to sing at his theatre f Lumley. Gye was aware of Mi Lumley sued Gye.

Legal principle
The court held th~~e~~

Key case and key statutory provision boxes – Identify the essential cases and statutes that you need to know for your exams.

KEY STATUTORY PROVISION

TULRCA 1992, s. 219

(1) An act done by a person in contemplation or furth~~er~~ dispute is not actionable in tort on the ground onl~~y~~

(a) that it induces another person to break a contract~~,~~ another person to interfere with its performance,

(b) that it consists in his threatening that a contract (is a party or not) will be broken or its performanc~~e~~ he will induce another person to break a contract performance.

Further thinking boxes – Illustrate areas of academic debate, and point you towards that extra reading required for the top grades.

FURTHER THINKING

Judicial and academic commentators have criticised the 'range of reasonable responses' test and the hurdles which it places in front of dismissed employees. Do you agree with Collins that 'in practice, it often degenerates into a test of perversity… [and] upholds the justice of dismissals that are "harsh but fair" '?

▮ H. Collins (2000) 'Finding the Right Direction for the Industrial Jury', 29 *Industrial Law Journal* 288

▮ H. Collins (2004) *Nine Proposals for the Reform of the Law on Unfair Dismissal.* London: Institute of Employment Rights.

Glossary – Forgotten the meaning of a word? Where a word is highlighted in the text, turn to the glossary at the back of the book to remind yourself of its meaning.

Glossary of terms

Key definitions

Fixed-term contract	A contract which endures for a specific period of time terminates at the end of that period of time.
Implied term of mutual trust and confidence	A term of the contract of employment that each party v not, without reasonable and proper cause, act in such as would be calculated or likely to destroy or seriously damage the relationship of trust and confidence existin between it and the other party to the contract.
Independent trade	A trade union which is not under the domination or co

Exam tips – Want to impress examiners? These indicate how you can improve your exam performance and your chances of getting top marks.

EXAM TIP

In answering essay questions, you should bear in mind the key idea that the implied duty of trust and confidence operates in a way to regulate the abuse or arbitrary use of power or discretion by an employer. In addition, the implied duty may be breached where the employer engages in a course of conduct or a series of actions or omissions, which cumulatively amount to a breach of duty. In answering problem questions, you should look out for employer's decisions which look like an abuse or arbitrary use of power (e.g. the removal of a bonus without consultation, the variation of key contractual terms or benefits without prior consultation, etc).

Revision notes – Highlight points that you should be aware of in other topic areas, or where your course may adopt a specific approach that you should check with your course tutor before reading further.

REVISION NOTE

The statutory right of a worker to be paid the national minimum wage should be taken into account when considering the implied duty of the employer to pay the employee wages even where there is no work. Provided the employee is ready and willing to work, payment will be due by the employer at the minimum wage.

Table of cases and statutes

Cases

Statutes

Secondary Legislation

EC law

Treaties and Conventions

1

The sources and institutions of employment law and key definitions

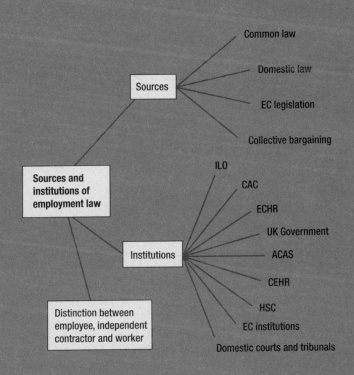

Sources
- Common law
- Domestic law
- EC legislation
- Collective bargaining

Sources and institutions of employment law

Institutions
- ILO
- CAC
- ECHR
- UK Government
- ACAS
- CEHR
- HSC
- EC institutions
- Domestic courts and tribunals

Distinction between employee, independent contractor and worker

Revision Checklist

What you need to know:

☐ The sources of employment law

☐ The institutions of employment law

☐ Distinction between an 'employee' and an 'independent contractor'

☐ An understanding of the 'worker' and 'contract personally to execute work or labour' categories

☐ Relationship between each of the categories.

Introduction:
Understanding sources and institutions of employment law and the definition of an 'employee'

Employment law has a number of sources and specific institutions and employment rights are available to employees, workers and independent contractors who have entered into a 'contract personally to execute work or labour'.

There are three sections to this chapter:

▮ the sources of employment law;
▮ the institutions of employment law; and
▮ an analysis of the concepts of 'employee', 'worker' and independent contractors who have entered into contracts 'personally to execute work or labour'.

Essay question advice

In connection with the sources and institutions of employment law, essays require broad general knowledge of those sources and institutions and their effect on the development of employment law and the enforcement of employment rights. You will also be expected to explain how legislation and the common law defines the key concepts of 'employee', 'worker' and the 'contract personally to execute work or labour'. An understanding of key cases in respect

▶

▶ of each of these concepts is required. You must also exhibit a knowledge of the employment rights enjoyed by 'employees', 'workers' and certain categories of self-employed persons. In tackling essay questions, you should always directly answer the question(s) asked and apply the relevant law.

Problem question advice

Problem questions concentrating on the sources and institutions of employment law may be framed in such a way that you are asked to advise the employee regarding the source of the rights available to them (e.g. rights based on domestic legislation, rights enshrined in domestic legislation which are based on EC law, rights having EC law directly as their source) and the competing prospects of success in raising a claim based on these sources in an employment tribunal, or a legal action in the courts. Most problem questions on the concepts of 'employee' and 'worker' will involve an examination of a person's relationship with an enterprise and whether it amounts to an 'employee' working under a contract of employment, a 'worker' or an independent contractor who has entered into a 'contract personally to execute work or labour'. In answering problem questions, you will require to discuss the relevant statutory definitions and common law tests which distinguish between these categories. This may also be combined with other areas of employment law (e.g. if the person is a 'worker', what employment rights do they enjoy). In tackling problem questions, you should always directly answer the question(s) asked and apply the relevant law to the facts at hand.

Sample question

Could you answer this question? Below is a typical essay question that could arise on this topic. Guidelines on answering the question are included at the end of the chapter, whilst a sample problem question and guidance on tackling it can be found on the companion website.

Essay question

Analyse how the law distinguishes between persons working under a contract of service and independent contractors. What is the legal significance of this distinction and is the law in need of reform?

■ Sources of employment law

With the exception of Chapter 11, this revision guide is concerned with the individual rights of **employees**, **workers** and independent contractors who have entered into contracts *'personally to execute work or labour'* – which are directly enforceable against employers. The sources of employment law and employment rights are diverse. The topic map outlines the key (but not all) sources of individual employment law. One of the most important sources is EC law. EC law provides employees, workers and certain self-employed persons/independent contractors with employment rights directly enforceable in the UK courts and tribunals via the Treaty of Amsterdam, EC Regulations and the decisions of the European Court of Justice. EC Directives provide employment rights directly in the national courts when domestic legislation implementing the terms of a Directive has come into force.

■ Institutions of employment law

There are a number of distinctive institutions of employment law. Some are designed to enforce and resolve employment disputes, such as the domestic courts, Employment Tribunals, the Employment Appeal Tribunal, CAC, the European Court of Human Rights and the European Court of Justice. Others are intended to act as institutions that prevent such disputes arising in the first place, such as ACAS and the CEHR. Some act as standard-setters, such as the International Labour Organization and ACAS (Codes of Practice), while others act as rule-makers, such as the European Commission, the European Parliament, the EC Council of Ministers and the UK Government. (See the topic map.)

Employment Tribunals and the Employment Appeal Tribunal

Specific mention must be made of the Employment Tribunals ('ETs') and the Employment Appeal Tribunal ('EAT'). ETs are specialist tribunals comprised of one qualified lawyer and two lay persons. One lay person is selected after consultation with employers' organisations. The other lay person is appointed after consultation with trade unions. The ETs are inferior courts and they are designed to be informal and cheaper for the public to use than domestic courts. ETs resolve employment law disputes which have legislation as their source. However, there are limited rights to raise employment claims before the ET where the dispute has the common law as its source. The constitutional basis and procedures of ETs are contained within the Employment Tribunals (Constitution and Rules of Procedure) Regulations 2004. Meanwhile, the EAT is comprised of divisions with hearings taking place in London or

Figure 1.1

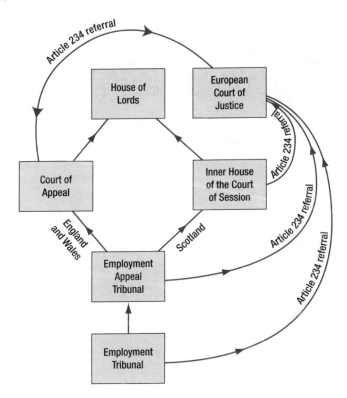

Edinburgh. The EAT is staffed with judges of the High Court in England or Senators of the College of Justice in the Court of Session in Scotland. Such judges or Senators must have experience or an understanding of employment law and employment relations. The EAT hears appeals from the ETs on points of employment law, inter alia. See Figure 1.1 for a flowchart of the channel of appeals and how an Article 234 referral may be made to the European Court of Justice.

■ Distinction between an 'employee', 'worker' and 'independent contractor'

'Employees' are entitled to the full suite of common law and statutory employment rights. 'Workers' and certain categories of self-employed persons/independent contractors enjoy varying degrees of limited employment rights.

Is an individual an 'employee'?

The courts have developed a number of tests to distinguish an 'employee' from an independent contractor.

Employment Rights Act 1996 ('ERA'), s. 230(1) and the Trade Union and Labour Relations (Consolidation) Act 1992 ('TULRCA'), s. 295(1)

An 'employee' is

'an individual who has entered into or works under . . . a contract of employment'.

ERA, s. 230(2) and TULRCA, s. 295(1)

In this Act 'contract of employment' means a 'contract of service . . . whether express or implied and (if it is express) whether oral or in writing'.

Common law tests for establishing 'contract of service'

No further statutory guidance is provided as to how the courts determine whether a 'contract of service' exists. Hence, the common law has established a number of tests for ascertaining whether an individual is undertaking work on the basis of a contract of employment:

■ The 'integration' test. Here, the courts enquire whether the work of the individual is an integral part of the business or organisation of the employer. If the answer is yes, then this is a factor in favour of the individual being an employee. See *Stevenson, Jordan & Harrison Ltd* v. *Macdonald & Evans* (1952).
■ The 'economic reality' test. This involves asking whether the individual is not working for his own account. If the answer is yes, this is a factor in favour of the individual being an employee. See *Market Investigations Ltd* v. *Minister of Social Security* (1969).
■ The 'mutuality of obligation' test. Here, one asks whether there is an obligation on

the part of the enterprise to offer a minimum or reasonable amount of work to the individual and whether there is an obligation on the individual to undertake a minimum amount of work. If the answer is yes, then this is a factor in favour of the individual being an employee. See *Carmichael* v. *National Power plc* (2000).

█ The 'control' test:

KEY CASE

Ready Mixed Concrete v. *Minister of Pensions and National Insurance* [1968] 1 All ER 433

Concerning: contract of employment, 'control' test

Facts

A yardman batcher entered into a new contract with a company which made and sold concrete. The contract involved the carriage of concrete and a dispute emerged regarding the status of the individual.

Legal principle

In order for a contract of service to exist, each of the following must be present:

1. the individual must provide his own work and exercise skill in the performance of his work in return for wages or other remuneration;
2. the individual must subject himself to the control of the other to a sufficient degree; and
3. the other provisions of the contract must be consistent with a contract of service.

As for the meaning of 'control', it includes the power of deciding the thing to be done, the way in which it shall be done, the means to be employed in doing it, the time when, and the place where it shall be done.

The 'multiple' test

In coming to a view as to whether an individual is an employee, the courts and tribunals now apply a 'multiple' test. In other words, they take into account each of the above four tests and a number of other factors. The greater the number of tests which have been satisfied and the greater the number of factors present, the more likely it is that the individual will be an employee. The relevant factors are as follows:

█ Does the contract give the individual no absolute right to send along a substitute to provide the work? If the answer is yes, then the more likely it is that the individual is an employee.

█ Is the individual paid wages or a salary rather than a fee, commission or royalties? If yes, then the more likely it is that the individual is an employee.

- Has the individual invested no capital in his work and does he suffer no risk of loss? If yes, then the more likely it is that the individual is an employee.
- Does the enterprise provide the individual's tools, uniform, stationery, equipment or materials? If yes, then the more likely it is that the individual is an employee.
- Does the individual pay income tax and NICs as an employee rather than charge VAT on their services or pay income tax and NICs as an independent contractor? If yes, then the more likely it is that the individual is an employee.
- Does the enterprise have the power to suspend, discipline or dismiss the individual or initiate or respond to disciplinary or grievance procedures? If yes, then the more likely it is that the individual is an employee.
- What label have the parties attached to their relationship? This will not be definitive, but may be relevant in a borderline case – see *Massey* v. *Crown Life Insurance* (1978).

Basic ingredients for contract of employment

Although the courts and tribunals apply the multiple test, what is clear is that if any of the following three criteria are absent, then the courts will hold that the individual concerned is not an employee:

- control;
- mutuality of obligation; and
- a degree of personal service on the part of the individual providing services.

The above three factors represent the 'irreducible minimum criteria' (i.e. the basic ingredients) which the courts require to be present.

KEY CASE

Montgomery v. *Johnson Underwood Ltd* [2001] IRLR 269

Concerning: contract of employment, basic ingredients

Facts

Montgomery was registered as an agency worker with Johnson Underwood ('the agency') and was placed with a client company of the agency. There was a dispute as to whether the agency or the client company was her employer.

Legal principle

Montgomery was not the employee of the agency or the client company. The Court of Appeal held that 'mutuality of obligation' and 'control' represented the irreducible minimum required for the establishment of a contract of employment. The fact that there was insufficient control on the part of the agency in this case meant that Montgomery could not be its employee.

KEY CASE

***Carmichael* v. *National Power plc* [2000] IRLR 43**

Concerning: the status of 'casual – as required' workers.

Facts

On the basis of a letter, Carmichael was appointed as a tour guide on a 'casual as required basis'. There were no set hours of work and payment was made at an hourly rate for work actually done, after deduction of income tax and national insurance. After a period of time, Carmichael complained that she was an employee.

Legal principle

Taking into account the terms of the letter, the oral exchanges between the parties, the surrounding circumstances and the subsequent conduct of the parties, it was clear that there was no mutuality of obligation present in the relationship. Accordingly, Mrs Carmichael was not an employee. The arrangement between the parties was flexible in that there was no intention to create an employment relationship which subsisted when Mrs Carmichael was not working.

Atypical workers

In the past 30 years, businesses have demanded and obtained more and more flexibility in the labour market. Organisations are keen to hire intermittent labour to meet market demands and offload labour as cheaply as possible when it is no longer needed. *Carmichael* demonstrates the issues which can arise when an individual providing work to an organisation is an 'atypical' worker. A typical worker can be defined as someone who provides work:

■ on the basis of a permanent contract,
■ for a single, identifiable employer,
■ at that employer's premises,
■ regardless of whether the employer has work or no work to provide.

In the case of an atypical worker, one of these four criteria is missing. Atypical workers come in a variety of shapes and sizes:

■ casual workers – who are engaged to provide work like Carmichael on a 'zero-hours' or a 'freelance' basis. Such workers may be asked to provide work only when the organisation requires them. When there is no work, they take the risk of the shortage of work;
■ agency workers like Montgomery who are hired out to a client company via an employment agency;

■ fixed-term workers (e.g. seasonal workers employed on short-term contracts);
■ part-time workers;
■ homeworkers (who work at home).

The main difficulty with atypical workers is that they are often dependent workers in a position of subordination vis-à-vis the organisation that engages them to provide work. However, they are more often than not unlikely to be held by the courts and/or tribunals to be employees by virtue of the absence of any mutuality of obligation or control.

EXAM TIP

In an essay question or problem question, look out for any assertion in the question that the individual has no obligation to accept an offer of work from an organisation – or that an organisation has no absolute obligation to offer a minimum or reasonable amount of work to an individual. Here, you should be discussing the 'mutuality of obligation' criterion, what this means and the legal implications of its absence.

Is an individual a 'worker'?

If an individual is not an employee, then they are likely to be an independent contractor. However, before coming to this conclusion, it is appropriate to consider whether they are a 'worker', since persons falling within this category will enjoy the employment rights listed in Figure 1.2.

KEY STATUTORY PROVISION
ERA, s. 230(3), National Minimum Wage Act 1998, s. 54(3) and the Working Time Regulations 1998, reg. 1
In this Act 'worker' means an individual who has entered into or works under ... (a) a contract of employment, or (b) any other contract ... whereby the individual undertakes to do or perform personally any work or services for another party to the contract whose status is not by virtue of the contract that of a client or customer of any profession or business undertaking carried on by the individual.

The key components of the 'worker' contract

In order to constitute a 'worker', an individual providing services to another must show the following three factors:

■ the presence of mutuality of obligation;
■ personal service on the part of the individual providing the services to another; and

Figure 1.2

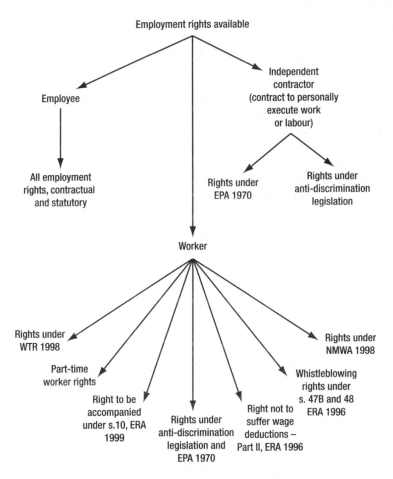

■ that the recipient of the services is not the client or customer of the individual providing the services.

REVISION NOTE

It is clear that the presence of 'mutuality of obligation' lies at the heart of the existence of both an employment contract and a 'worker' contract.

Is the individual an independent contractor who enjoys certain limited employment rights?

If an individual is neither an 'employee' nor a 'worker', then they are an independent contractor. However, this does not mean that they enjoy no employment rights at all. Certain self-employed persons who enter contracts 'personally to execute work or labour' do have the benefit of certain employment rights: for example, the anti-discrimination and equal pay rights under anti-discrimination legislation and the Equal Pay Act 1970.

KEY STATUTORY PROVISION

Equal Pay Act 1970, s. 1(6)(a), Sex Discrimination Act 1975, s. 82(1), Race Relations Act 1976, s. 78(1) and the Disability Discrimination Act 1995, s. 68(1)

'employment' means employment under a contract of service . . . or *a contract personally to execute any work or labour . . .*' [emphasis added]

KEY CASE

Mingeley v. Pennock and Ivory t/a Amber Cars **[2004] IRLR 373**

Concerning: 'contract personally to execute any work or labour'

Facts

Mingeley was of black African origin. He worked as a private hire taxi driver; he owned the car he used for that purpose. By contract with Amber Cars, he paid £75.00 a week for access to its radio and computer system, which allocated calls to drivers. He kept the fares he collected. The Race Relations Act 1976 confers anti-discrimination rights in favour of an individual who enters into a 'contract personally to execute any work or labour'. The question was whether Mingeley satisfied this definition.

Legal principle

The Court of Appeal held that for a person to be employed under a contract personally to execute any work or labour there required to be mutual obligations to offer or accept work. Since this was not present, Mingeley did not satisfy the definition in s. 78(1) of the Race Relations Act 1976.

The nature of the 'worker' contract and the 'contract personally to execute any work or labour'

What is clear about the definition of the 'worker' and the 'contract personally to execute any work or labour' is that, like the definition of 'employee', there is a requirement for:

■ mutuality of obligation; and
■ a contract personally to provide a service by one party to another.

Two points can be made here:

■ if a contract gives the individual the *absolute* power to send along a substitute to perform the work, they will not satisfy the definitions of 'worker' and 'contract personally to execute any work or labour'; and
■ the 'contract personally to execute any work or labour' is wider than the 'worker' contract. In the case of the latter, one must enquire whether the recipient of the individual's services is a client or customer of the individual concerned. This means that individuals providing services personally to clients or customers are not covered. In contrast, in the case of the 'contract personally to execute any work or labour', the individual concerned may be providing services personally to clients or customers – yet be covered by the legislation.

FURTHER THINKING

Commentators in favour of restructuring the employment relationship and moving away from the model of the contract of employment advocate a codified structure – akin to status over contract. On the other side of the debate are those who favour the retention of the existing contractual model, albeit in a (radically) reformed guise. For example, Freedland is of the view that employment law should continue to be predicated on contract law.

■ B. Hepple (1986) 'Restructuring Employment Rights', 15 *Industrial Law Journal* 69.
■ M. Freedland (2006) 'From the Contract of Employment to the Personal Work Nexus', 35(1) *Industrial Law Journal* 1.

▌Chapter summary
▌Putting it all together

TEST YOURSELF

☐ Can you tick all the points from the revision checklist at the beginning of this chapter?

☐ Take the **end-of-chapter quiz** on the companion website.

☐ Test your knowledge of the cases below with the **revision flashcards** on the website.

☐ Attempt the essay question at the beginning of the chapter using the guidelines below.

☐ Go to the companion website to try out other questions.

Answer guidelines

See the essay question at the start of this chapter. A diagram illustrating how to structure your answer is available on the website.

Points to remember when answering this question:

▋ An introduction should be included which explains the changes in the structure of the underlying labour market and economy and the shift away from rigid permanent employment towards atypical working relationships.

▋ Differentiate between the contract of employment, the contract for services, the 'worker' contract and the 'contract personally to execute any work or labour'.

▋ Address the various tests which are applied, and have been applied, by the courts to determine the status of an individual providing services. What are the minimum criteria which must be present for the existence of a contract of employment?

Make your answer stand out

▋ Address the academic debates regarding the appropriateness of the contractual model at the heart of the employment relationship, the 'worker' contract and the 'contract personally to execute work or labour'.

▋ Explore the possible path and future development of the employment relationship. Is the law flexible enough to evolve to cater for atypical working relationships?

2

Implied terms of the contract of employment (1): duties of the employer

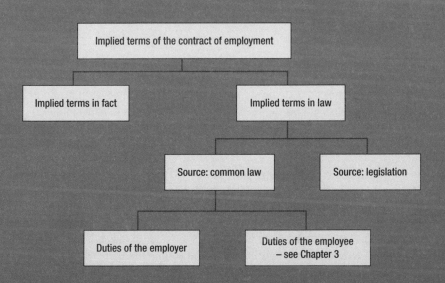

Implied terms of the contract of employment

Implied terms in fact

Implied terms in law

Source: common law

Source: legislation

Duties of the employer

Duties of the employee – see Chapter 3

Revision Checklist

What you need to know:

- [ ] The different types of implied duties imposed on an employer
- [ ] The sources of the implied duties
- [ ] The circumstances under which an employer will be in breach of duty in failing to provide an employee with work
- [ ] The different types of sub-duties imposed on an employer pursuant to the overall duty to exercise reasonable care
- [ ] The content, nature and scope of the employer's duty to maintain trust and confidence.

Introduction:
Understanding the employer's implied duties

By operation of law, an employer owes a number of diverse implied duties to an employee.

This chapter concentrates on the implied terms of the contract of employment. The implied terms of the contract of employment can be divided into (1) those implied terms which can be seen as imposing implied duties on an employer in favour of an employee and (2) those implied terms which can be viewed as imposing implied duties on an employee in favour of the employer. In Chapter 2 we will concentrate on the employer's implied duties and in Chapter 3 we will consider the employee's implied duties.

The implied duties arise by operation of law by virtue of the fact that the employer and employee have entered into a contract of employment. For this reason, the implied terms in law can be distinguished from implied terms in fact. Implied terms in law are implied into every contract of employment. However, implied terms in fact are not implied into every contract of employment as a matter of law, but are case-specific implied terms which are introduced into a contract of employment in a particular case in order to give it 'business efficacy'.

The sources of the implied duties are (i) the common law and (ii) legislation. However, some of the implied duties having the common law as their source have been influenced by legislation.

Essay question advice

Essays require broad general knowledge of the implied duties of the employer. In particular, the examiner may be looking for an examination of the development of the implied duties and whether the current position is satisfactory. In addressing the broader aspects of the implied duties, the examiner will also expect you to address the sources, content, nature and scope of application of the implied duties. In tackling essay questions, you should always directly answer the question(s) asked and apply the relevant law.

Problem question advice

Problem questions may involve an examination of more than one of the implied duties of the employer. This may also be combined with other areas of employment law. For example,

- the implied duties of the employee; and
- in the case of the employer's implied duty to pay wages/remunerate, the effect of the National Minimum Wage Act 1998 and the prohibitions on the unauthorised deductions of wages on this duty in Part II of the Employment Rights Act 1996 ('ERA').

Problem questions concentrating on the implied duties of an employer may be framed in such a way that you will be asked to advise the employee whether they have a reasonable prospect of success in raising a claim in an employment tribunal, or a legal action in the courts. In tackling problem questions, you should always directly answer the question(s) asked and apply the relevant law to the facts at hand.

Sample question

Could you answer this question? Below is a typical problem question that could arise on this topic. Guidelines on answering the question are included at the end of the chapter, whilst a sample essay question and guidance on tackling it can be found on the companion website.

Problem question

Jonathan, a senior engineer, has been employed by an engineering company for seven years and consults you after he was told to go home by his employer at a recent meeting. His employer told him that they had no work to give him and would let him know as soon as work became available. At the meeting, Jonathan was also told by ▶

his employer that he would no longer receive the free shares in the employer's company which he had received every month in terms of his written contract of employment. On his way out of the meeting, Jonathan tripped over an unattended bucket of water (which he had not seen) and broke his leg. Advise Jonathan on the rights he enjoys in terms of the implied terms of his contract of employment.

■ Duty to provide work?

An employer is under no duty to provide an employee with work. However, the courts have created exceptions to this general rule in certain factual circumstances where the nature of the employee's work is so important that the employee requires to work at all times in order to:

■ maintain or develop key skill levels; or
■ keep up to date with developments in the industry, sector or trade within which they work.

Furthermore, an employer may also be under a duty to provide work where:

■ there was an understanding between the employer and employee that the employee would be given a reasonable amount of work in order that they could enjoy a certain level of earnings; or
■ the failure to provide the employee with work may lead to a loss of reputation or publicity on the part of the employee.

Much will depend on the facts and circumstances of the case.

Scope of exceptions

Students often find it difficult to understand fully how the exceptions to the general rule apply. Where they apply, the employer is under a duty to provide an employee with work. The exceptions fall broadly within four types: see Figure 2.1 for guidance.

Figure 2.1

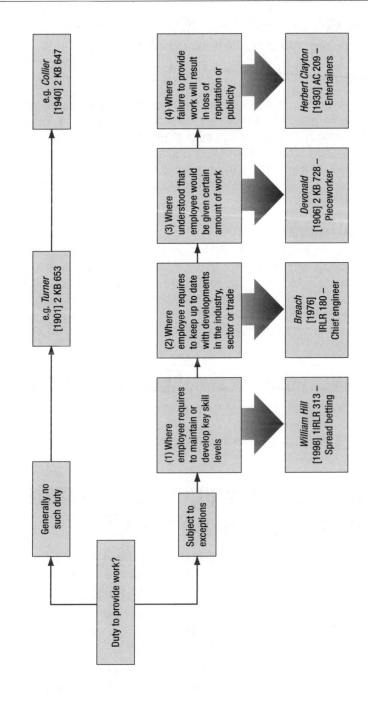

William Hill Organisation Ltd v. Tucker [1998] 1 IRLR 313

Concerning: duty to provide work, exception

Facts

The employer of a senior dealer in a spread betting business requested that he go on 'garden leave' when the dealer served notice that he was terminating his contract of employment to take up fresh employment with a competitor of the employer. 'Garden leave' describes the situation where an employer requires an employee not to work during the period of notice of termination of employment, subject to the continued receipt of all other contractual benefits, including salary, during that period.

Legal principle

In the case of a highly skilled employee (such as Mr Tucker), in the absence of a clause in the contract of employment, garden leave will not be possible. Accordingly, Mr Tucker was entitled to be provided with work during the notice period. Note that, if the employee had not been highly skilled, this case suggests that the employer would have been able to put him on garden leave, whether or not an express term to that effect had been inserted in his written contract.

EXAM TIP

In a problem question, look out for an employee who is described as a 'professional', 'salesman', 'engineer', 'entertainer', 'actor' or 'performer'. In such questions, you should immediately think of the exceptions to the general rule.

Duty to pay wages/remunerate when there is no work?

Where an employee is not undertaking work, but is ready and willing to work, they will be entitled to be paid and remunerated. However, there are exceptions to this general rule. For example, in the absence of an express term to the contrary, the employer may legally withhold wages:

■ where the employer requires to close down a place of business through no fault of its own (e.g. *Browning* v. *Crumlin Valley Collieries Ltd* (1926)); or
■ an employee is absent due to ill-health.

In the second case above, the employee remains entitled to statutory sick pay.

Ill-health

Complications arise where an employee is absent from work due to long-term sickness. In terms of social security law, an employee who is ill and absent from work is entitled to be paid statutory sick pay. However, statutory sick pay is capped at a rather low figure. Therefore, the question is whether an employee is entitled to be paid their full wages over and above the statutory sick pay. If the contract of employment is silent, the case of *Mears* v. *Safecar Security Ltd* (1983) demonstrates that the answer to this question will be negative, unless the employee can point to some implied term to the contrary.

EXAM TIP

The area of the payment of wages to, and the remuneration of, employees is influenced by legislation. First, the National Minimum Wage Act 1998 sets a minimum threshold on the amount of wages which can be paid to employees in a working hour. Second, the terms of Part II of the ERA control the extent to which an employer may make unauthorised deductions from the wages of employees. Third, the law of constructive dismissal, in terms of Part X of the ERA, regulates the extent to which an employer can unilaterally vary the express terms of the contract of employment concerning the payment of wages and other contractual benefits. Fourth, s. 28 of the ERA affects the payment of remuneration to employees by conferring statutory guarantee pay in certain circumstances.

■ Duty in respect of discretionary bonuses?

The employer is under an implied duty to exercise a discretion to pay a discretionary bonus in a manner which is bona fide and rational. A refusal to make a discretionary bonus payment will amount to a breach of the implied duty if no employer would have exercised that discretion in that way: that is the decision was perverse, irrational or contrary to good faith. See *Horkulak* v. *Cantor Fitzgerald Ltd* (2004).

■ Duty to indemnify employee in respect of expenses reasonably incurred?

An employee is entitled to be reimbursed by the employer in respect of any costs and expenses the former incurs in performing his employment duties.

■Duty to exercise reasonable care for the employee's physical and psychological well-being?

An employer is under a duty to exercise reasonable care in respect of the employee's physical and psychological well-being. This duty is a contractual duty, but its content is heavily influenced by the duty of care in negligence in the law of tort and delict (in Scotland). Therefore, whether an employer has breached the implied duty to exercise reasonable care depends on whether the employer has discharged the relevant standard of care and taken the necessary steps. If the employer has not reached the

Figure 2.2

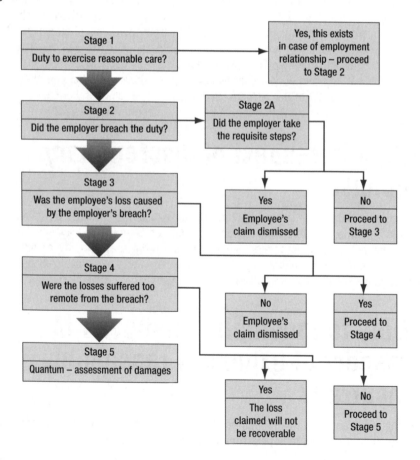

requisite standard of care, the court will hold that the implied duty has been breached. Issues of causation, remoteness of damage and quantum will equally be relevant in the law of the contract of employment and in the law of tort or delict (in Scotland). See Figure 2.2 for a breakdown of the relevant stages.

Content and nature of the implied duty

The implied duty to exercise reasonable care can be divided into three sub-duties:

■ the employer's duty to provide safe plant, equipment, tools, materials and appliances in the workplace;
■ the employer's duty to provide a safe and secure system of work;
■ the employer's duty to provide the employee with reasonably competent fellow employees.

Figure 2.3

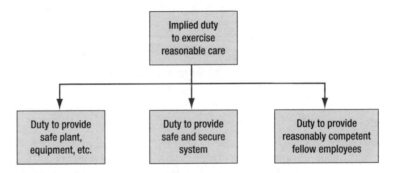

KEY CASE

***Wilsons & Clyde Coal Co. Ltd* v. *English* [1938] AC 57**

Concerning: duty to exercise reasonable care, physical well-being

Facts

An employee was killed as a result of an accident at work. The employer argued that the duty to provide a safe system of work had been delegated to a competent employee and that it was not liable.

Legal principle

The House of Lords held that the implied duty was personal to the employer. It could not be devolved upon one of its employees. Therefore, the employer could be held liable for negligence in the performance or discharge of that implied duty to exercise reasonable care.

EXAM TIP

In an essay question or problem question, look out for any assertion that there is an express term in the contract of employment to the effect that the weekly working hours of the employee may exceed 48 hours at the option or discretion of the employer. A question like this is looking for you to discuss the following:

1. the extent to which the implied terms of the contract of employment may overrule the express terms of that contract; and
2. the effect of reg. 4(1) and (2) of the Working Time Regulations 1998 (SI 1998/1833) on the implied duty.

With regard to 1, in *Johnstone* v. *Bloomsbury Health Authority* (1991) it was held that the employer's implied duty to exercise reasonable care may overrule the employer's exercise of discretion based upon the express contractual powers of the employer. In relation to 2, reg 4(1) of the Working Time Regulations 1998 enables an employee and employer to opt out of the employee's right not to work in excess of 48 hours in a working week. If the employee provides their agreement in writing to waive such a right, the agreement is effective. See Chapter 4 for further details.

KEY CASE

Johnstone v. *Bloomsbury Health Authority* [1991] IRLR 118

Concerning: duty to exercise reasonable care, express terms, psychiatric well-being

Facts

An employee was employed as a junior doctor by a hospital. His written contract of employment provided that his standard working week was 40 hours. However, his employer had a discretion to call on him to work an extra 48 hours a week on average. Some weeks, it was alleged, the employee was working in excess of 100 hours. The consequence was that he suffered from stress and depression.

Legal principle

The Court of Appeal held that the employer's implied duty to exercise reasonable care is capable of overruling the employer's exercise of discretion based upon the express contractual powers of the employer. Thus, the exercise of the employer's option to call on the employee to work a further 48 hours per week was controlled and regulated by the content of the implied duty. However, one should be clear that this is not the same as saying that the implied duty cuts down or ousts the express term. Instead, as Lord Browne-Wilkinson stated, the scope of the employer's implied duty requires to be carved with reference to the express terms of the contract so that they can co-exist: that is the express term will fashion and influence the normative content of the implied duty and the standard of care, but will not supersede it.

REVISION NOTE

In Chapter 3, we will examine the implied duties of the employee. An employee is also under an implied duty to exercise skill and care in the performance of their contractual duties.

The requisite standard of care

As Figure 2.2 demonstrates, whether the employer has breached the implied duty to exercise reasonable care depends on whether it took the requisite steps necessary to satisfy the standard of care. The standard of care and the nature and content of those steps will depend on the context and the circumstances of the case. If the standard of care is met by the employer, the court will hold that it has not breached the implied duty. If the employer has failed to meet the requisite standard, the court will hold that the employer has breached the implied duty.

Examples of breach

Figure 2.4

Case name	Breach
Pagano [1976] IRLR 9	Unsafe vehicles
British Aircraft Corporation [1978] IRLR 332	Failure to provide eye protection
Graham Oxley, Tool Steels [1980] IRLR 135	Exposure to freezing working conditions
Waters [2000] IRLR 720	Failure to deal with complaint of sexual assualt
Waltons and Morse [1997] IRLR 488	Failure to deal with smoky working environment

Psychiatric injury

In *Walker* v. *Northumberland County Council* (1995), it was settled that the employer's implied duty to exercise reasonable care extends to the psychiatric well-being of the employee. A claimant employee must show that they are suffering from a recognised psychiatric illness which is attributable to the workplace. In *Sutherland* v. *Hatton* (2002), the Court of Appeal outlined 16 practical propositions which govern:

■ whether the employer has breached the implied duty; and
■ the issue of causation in the context of psychiatric harm.

You should familiarise yourself with these 16 propositions. In *Barber* v. *Somerset County Council* (2004), the House of Lords approved these 16 guidelines as useful rules of thumb, but stated that they should not be treated as the equivalent of a statute. In *Hartman* v. *South Essex Mental Health and Community Care NHS Trust* (2005), the Court of Appeal gave judgment in six appealed cases, by applying the guidance in *Sutherland*.

EXAM TIP

In problem questions, look out for any suggestion of an employee suffering from depression, anxiety or stress. Here, you should be thinking about the employer's implied duty to exercise reasonable care for the psychiatric well-being of the employee in the question. You should apply the guidelines in *Sutherland*, remembering that the employee must be suffering from a recognised psychiatric illness which is attributable to the workplace if their claim is to be successful.

■ Duty to exercise reasonable care for the employee's economic and financial well-being?

An employer is under no implied duty to exercise reasonable care for the economic and financial well-being of its employees. Where:

■ a particular term of the contract of employment makes available to the employee a valuable right; and
■ that right is contingent upon the employee taking action to avail himself of its benefit; and
■ the employee could not, in all the circumstances, reasonably be expected to be aware of the term unless it was drawn to his attention,

there is no general implied duty on the part of the employer to take reasonable steps to bring it to the attention of the employee.

Such an implied duty may be owed, but this will depend on the facts and circumstances of the case and will not be implied as a matter of law in every contract of employment. This point was settled in *Crossley* v. *Faithful & Gould Holdings Ltd* (2004), despite earlier indications to the contrary in the House of Lords in *Spring* v. *Guardian Assurance plc* (1995) and *Scally* v. *Southern Health and Social Services Board* (1992). The exception is the situation dealt with in *Spring*, where it was held that an employer is under an implied duty to exercise reasonable care and skill in producing a reference.

■ Duty to co-operate?

An employee is under a duty to co-operate with his or her employer – see Chapter 3. It was always thought that this duty was not reciprocal. However, the recent case of *Takacs* v. *Barclays Services Jersey Ltd* (2006) would suggest otherwise. In *Takacs*, Master Fontaine in the High Court held that an employee had a prospect of succeeding in his claim that there was an implied term in his contract of employment that his employers would co-operate with him in fulfilling the condition for payment of the additional awards attached to a contractually guaranteed bonus. Whether this duty to co-operate will be recognised by higher authority is difficult to answer at this stage.

■ Duty to maintain and preserve trust and confidence?

An employer owes a duty to its employees to maintain and preserve the trust and confidence inherent within the employment relationship. This implied term is mutual – it imposes an implied duty of trust and confidence on an employer and an implied duty of trust and confidence on an employee. The implied duty confers rights on the party to whom the implied duty is owed.

KEY DEFINITION
Implied term of mutual trust and confidence: A term of the contract of employment that each party will not, without reasonable and proper cause, act in such a way as would be calculated or likely to destroy or seriously damage the relationship of trust and confidence existing between it and the other party to the contract.

KEY CASE

Malik v. *BCCI* [1997] IRLR 462

Concerning: implied duty of mutual trust and confidence, example of breach

Facts

A number of employees raised claims against their employer on the basis that the employer had breached an implied duty to maintain and preserve the trust and confidence inherent within the employment relationship. It was alleged that this implied duty existed as a matter of law and had been breached by the employer.

▶

KEY CASE

Legal principle

The House of Lords held that there was an implied term of the contract of employment that trust and confidence inherent in the employment relationship should be maintained and preserved. Translated into the language of implied duties, this imposes reciprocal duties on the employer and the employee to maintain such trust and confidence.

Controlling dismissal and suspension

In the cases of *Johnson* v. *Unisys Ltd* (2001) and *Eastwood* v. *Magnox Electric plc* (2004), the House of Lords held that the implied term could not be used to control or regulate the exercise of an employer's discretionary power to dismiss an employee. However, in *Gogay* v. *Hertfordshire CC* (2000) the Court of Appeal held that the implied term could be breached where an employer exercised its power to suspend an employee.

KEY CASE

Johnson v. _Unisys Ltd_ [2001] IRLR 279

Concerning: implied duty of mutual trust and confidence, dismissal

Facts

An employee was successful in his unfair dismissal claim against an employer in the employment tribunal. He was awarded the maximum compensation allowable under statute at that time. Two years later, he raised an action in court for damages. He claimed that he had been wrongfully dismissed by the employer in breach of the employer's implied duty of trust and confidence.

Legal principle

The House of Lords held that an employee will not be awarded damages on the basis of wrongful dismissal where it was claimed that the act or manner of the dismissal breached the employer's implied duty of trust and confidence.

EXAM TIP

In problem questions or essay questions, you should take care where the question involves an employee seeking to raise a claim for breach of the implied duty on the basis of the employer's act of dismissal or the manner of their dismissal. The law is clear in such situations to the effect that the implied duty will not be available to the employee to control that dismissal.

The law of wrongful dismissal is covered in Chapter 8. *Malik* v. *BCCI*, *Johnson* v. *Unisys Ltd* and *Eastwood* v. *Magnox Electric plc* have implications for the claims that may be raised by an employee under the umbrella of a wrongful dismissal action in a court.

The law of **constructive dismissal** is covered in Chapter 10. You must appreciate that the implied term of mutual trust and confidence – and whether this term has been breached – lies at the heart of many constructive dismissal claims. In *Western Excavating (ECC) Ltd* v. *Sharp* (1978) the Court of Appeal held that whether an employee had been constructively dismissed depended on whether the employer's conduct constituted a significant or repudiatory breach of contract going to the root of the contract of employment. Where the implied term of mutual trust and confidence is breached, this automatically amounts to a repudiatory breach – see *Morrow* v. *Safeway Stores plc* (2002).

Abuse of discretion or power

The implied duty is principally used by an employee where an employer has exercised its express or implicit discretion, power, option or right in a way which is capricious, arbitrary or represents an abuse. For an analysis of key cases, see Figure 2.5.

In answering essay questions, you should bear in mind the key idea that the implied duty of trust and confidence operates in a way to regulate the abuse or arbitrary use of power or discretion by an employer. In addition, the implied duty may be breached where the employer engages in a course of conduct or a series of actions or omissions, which cumulatively amount to a breach of duty. In answering problem questions, you should look out for employer's decisions which look like an abuse or arbitrary use of power (e.g. the removal of a bonus without consultation, the variation of key contractual terms or benefits without prior consultation, etc).

Figure 2.5

Case name	Legal principle
BG plc [2001] IRLR 496	Implied term not concerned with the reasonableness of the employer's conduct
Croft [2002] IRLR 851	The implied duty can be used to call omissions to account
Hagen [2002] IRLR 31	Single acts of negligence will not usually amount to a breach
Transco plc (formerly BG plc) [2002] IRLR 444	Implied duty concerned with the control of arbitrary or capricious use of discretionary powers
Omilaju [2005] IRLR 35	Implied duty is available to strike down a course of conduct
French [1998] IRLR 646	The employer's decision to remove or vary an employee's terms and conditions of employment is subject to review
Greenhof [2006] IRLR 98	A breach of an employer's statutory duty to make reasonable adjustments in terms of the DDA 1995 was a breach

FURTHER THINKING

The implied duty of trust and confidence is currently in an embryonic state. It continues to be developed piecemeal by the courts and tribunals on a case-by-case basis. The route of the implied term of mutual trust and confidence continues and its final destination is yet to be charted. The following writings of Brodie are extremely valuable reading:

▌ D. Brodie, (1998) 'Beyond Exchange: the New Contract of Employment' 27 *Industrial Law Journal* 79

▌ D. Brodie, (2001) 'Legal Coherence and the Employment Revolution' 117 *Law Quarterly Review* 604.

Chapter summary
Putting it all together

☐ Can you tick all the points from the revision checklist at the beginning of this chapter?

☐ Take the **end-of-chapter quiz** on the companion website.

☐ Test your knowledge of the cases below with the **revision flashcards** on the website.

☐ Attempt the essay question at the beginning of the chapter using the guidelines below.

☐ Go to the companion website to try out other questions.

Answer guidelines

See the problem question at the start of this chapter. A diagram illustrating how to structure your answer is available on the website.

Points to remember when answering this question:

▪ In your introduction, make the point that Jonathan has a number of heads of claim open to him.

▪ You should consider whether Jonathan has a claim on the basis that his employer has breached its implied duty to provide work – this will depend on the nature of his occupation.

▪ Consider the nature of Jonathan's claim in respect of the shares he is entitled to under his contract of employment. Is this right based on an implied term or an express term of the contract of employment?

▪ Jonathan's employer is in breach of its implied duty to exercise reasonable care for his physical well-being.

Make your answer stand out

▪ Consider whether there is scope for arguing that the implied term of mutual trust and confidence has been breached as a result of the actions of Jonathan's employer.

3
Implied terms of the contract of employment (2): duties of the employee

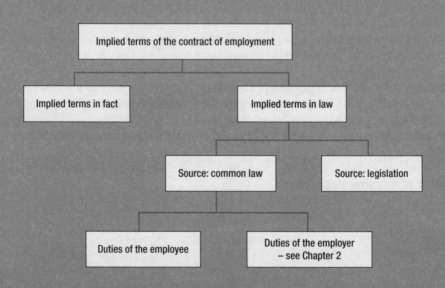

Revision Checklist

What you need to know:

☐ The different types of implied duties owed by an employee

☐ The sources of the employee's implied duties

☐ The circumstances in which an employee will be in breach of their duty to comply with the reasonable and lawful instructions of the employer

☐ The content, nature and scope of the employee's duty of fidelity and loyalty and the nature of the sub-duties which comprise the duty of fidelity and loyalty.

Introduction:
Understanding the employer's implied duties

By operation of law, an employee owes a number of diverse implied duties to an employer.

This chapter concentrates on the implied terms of the contract of employment. In Chapter 2 we considered the implied duties of the employer and in this chapter we will concentrate on the employee's implied duties.

The implied duties arise by operation of law by virtue of the fact that the employer and employee have entered into a contract of employment. The implied duties have (i) the common law and (ii) legislation as their source. In this chapter, we will consider the implied duties having the common law as their source only. We will also examine how these common-law-based implied duties have been influenced by legislation.

Essay question advice

Essays require broad general knowledge of the implied duties of the employee. In particular, the examiner will be looking for an examination of the development of the implied duties and whether the current position is satisfactory. The examiner may also expect you to address the sources, content, nature and scope of application of the implied duties. Since the implied duties are based on the common law, an understanding of key cases in respect of each of the implied duties will be expected. In tackling essay questions, you should always directly answer the question(s) asked and apply the relevant law.

Problem question advice

Most problem questions will involve an examination of more than one of the implied duties of the employee. This may also be combined with other areas of employment law. For example:

- the implied duties of the employer;
- the statutory duties of the employer or the employee; and/or
- the effect of the express terms of the contract of employment on the implied duties of the employee.

Problem questions concentrating on the implied duties of an employee may be framed in such a way that you are asked to advise the employee whether there is a reasonable prospect of success in raising a claim in an employment tribunal, or a legal action in the courts. In tackling problem questions, you should always directly answer the question(s) asked and apply the relevant law to the facts at hand.

Sample question

Could you answer this question? Below is a typical essay question that could arise on this topic. Guidelines on answering the question are included at the end of the chapter, whilst a sample problem question and guidance on tackling it can be found on the companion website.

Essay question

Critically evaluate the content and scope of the employee's implied duty of fidelity and loyalty.

■Duty to obey reasonable and lawful instructions and orders?

An employee is under a duty to comply with the reasonable and lawful instructions of their employer. However, the employee is excused from performance where the employer's instructions or orders are unreasonable or unlawful. There is also an exception to the general rule: an employee is not bound to follow the reasonable instructions or orders of the employer where this will expose the employee and others to unjustifiable risks.

KEY CASE

Pepper v. *Webb* [1969] 1 WLR 514

Concerning: implied duty to comply with reasonable and lawful instructions or orders of employer

Facts

Webb's wife appointed Mr Pepper as head gardener. An incident occurred after Webb's wife instructed Pepper to plant some plants. Pepper refused. Webb subsequently asked Pepper to plant the plants. Pepper again refused in strong terms. Thereupon, Webb summarily dismissed Pepper.

Legal principle

Webb and his wife's instructions were reasonable and lawful. Hence, Pepper was in repudiatory breach of contract in failing to comply with such instructions. Contrast the facts of this case with *Wilson* v. *Racher* (1974).

KEY CASE

Donovan v. *Invicta Airlines* [1970] 1 Lloyd's Rep 486

Concerning: exception, implied duty to comply with reasonable and lawful instructions or orders of employer

Facts

Donovan was a freelance air pilot. On a number of occasions, for the purposes of speed or economy, his employer:

1. invited him to fly contrary to regulations;
2. failed to maintain the aircraft in a safe condition; and
3. was discourteous to him.

Legal principle

The employer's instructions to fly the aircraft in such circumstances exposed the employee and others (e.g. passengers and the public) to unjustifiable risks. Accordingly, the employee had not breached his implied duty to comply with reasonable and lawful instructions or orders of the employer. Instead, the employer's conduct was such that it amounted to a repudiatory breach of the contract of employment.

Limitations on implied duty to obey reasonable and lawful instructions and orders

Students often fail to appreciate that the implied duty of the employee is subject to the statutory employment rights of employees. For example, an employee will not be in breach of the implied duty if they refuse an employer's instruction to perform a particular task on the basis that they are exercising their right to take a reasonable amount of time off from work to deal with a crisis relating to their dependants in terms of s. 57A of the Employment Rights Act 1996 ('ERA 1996'). Likewise, there is no breach of duty where an employee refuses an employer's instructions to work in excess of 48 hours in breach of reg. 4(1) of the Working Time Regulations 1998.

EXAM TIP

In a problem question, look out for any suggestion that an employee is being asked to comply with an instruction or order. You should then consider whether the instruction:

▪ is unlawful or unreasonable;
▪ exposes the employee to unjustifiable or unquantifiable risks; or
▪ is incompatible with an employee's statutory rights.

If so, the employee will be excused from performance.

■ Duty to indemnify their employer?

An employee is under an obligation to indemnify his employer where his actions result in loss to the employer.

■ Duty to exercise care and perform duties competently?

An employee has a duty to exercise the normal degree of skill and care in the performance of his work. An employee must also perform his duties in a competent manner. An employee should not follow the reasonable and lawful instructions or orders of the employer in a literal fashion which has the effect of disrupting the business of the employer, e.g. a 'work to rule' policy.

Lister v. Romford Ice and Cold Storage Co. Ltd [1957] AC 555

Concerning: implied duty to exercise care, breach

Facts

A lorry driver employee negligently drove his lorry, injuring his father who was a fellow employee. The employer was held to be vicariously liable for the actions of the lorry driver and so the father recovered damages from the employer. The employer then sued the lorry driver on the basis that the latter had breached this implied duty.

Legal principle

The employee had been in breach of duty. Hence, his employer was entitled to recover damages from him in the amount for which they had been made liable to his father.

Problem area

Where an employee causes an injury to a fellow employee, the injured employee can seek redress from the employer. This is based on the tortious or delictual (in Scotland) doctrine of vicarious liability, whereby the employer assumes liability for the negligent actions of the employee in the scope of the employee's employment. Thereafter, as occurred in *Lister*, an employer who has been held vicariously liable may seek indemnification from the negligent employee in respect of the losses which they sustained in paying out compensation to the injured employee. Whether the employer adopts such a course of action is essentially a matter for their insurers.

Secretary of State for Employment v. ASLEF [1972] 2 QB 443 and 455

Concerning: breach of implied duty to perform duties competently

Facts

Pursuant to an industrial dispute, three trade unions instructed their member employees to work strictly in accordance with their employer's rule book, i.e. 'work to rule' as a means of disrupting the employer's business.

Legal principle

The Court of Appeal held that the employees were breaching their contract of employment. It was held that each employee would not, in obeying lawful instructions, seek to carry them out in a manner which had the effect of disrupting the employer's business.

EXAM TIP

In an essay question or problem question, look out for any assertion in the question that the employees are complying with the strict letter of the employer's handbook or rule book, i.e. 'work to rule'. Where an employee does so, this will commonly have a depreciatory effect on the business of the employer in lost time and revenues. In each case, this will be a matter of fact and degree and you will be required to offer a reasoned view on this point.

Duty to adapt and co-operate?

Over time, an employer may restructure the methods of the workplace or the manner in which an employee is expected to perform their duties. Where these changes are adopted, an employee is expected to adapt and co-operate with the employer in the introduction of such changes. An employee will be in breach of duty if they fail to do so.

KEY CASE

Cresswell v. *Board of Inland Revenue* [1984] IRLR 190

Concerning: implied duty to adapt and co-operate with employer

Facts

The employer introduced a new computer system for the purposes of simplifying and rendering more efficient the method by which PAYE was calculated, administered and paid. A crisis ensued when the employees refused to use the new computer system and the employer withdrew permission from the employees to use the old system, refusing to pay them while they rejected it.

Legal principle

The employees were in breach of contract. An employee is under an obligation to adapt to new working methods and co-operate with the employer in introducing such systems or techniques.

Content and nature of the implied duty

It was recognised in *Cresswell* that it will be difficult to assess when a new working method, pattern or technique is so pronounced that it in fact represents a new job which the employee is being asked to perform. Where the changes are so great that the job description has effectively changed, the change will represent an attempt by the employer unilaterally to vary the terms of the employee's contract of employment.

In such circumstances, the employee will be relieved from their duty to adapt and co-operate. In *Cresswell*, it was held that it was a question of fact whether the introduction of new methods and techniques altered the nature of the work to such a degree that it was no longer the work that the employee had agreed to perform under the terms of his contract.

Duty to maintain and preserve trust and confidence?

The duty to maintain and preserve the trust and confidence inherent in the employment relationship is mutual. In this chapter, we consider the implied duty imposed on an employee which confers rights on an employer. Since the implied duty is mutual, its content, scope, nature and source is the same in any given case, regardless of whether it is the employer or employee who it is alleged owes or has breached the duty.

KEY CASE

Briscoe v. Lubrizol Limited [2002] IRLR 607

Concerning: implied duty to maintain trust and confidence, breach

Facts

An employee on long-term sick leave was being paid sums by insurers via his employer, in terms of a disability payment insurance scheme. The insurers subsequently rejected the employer's right to claim on behalf of the employee under the scheme. The employer corresponded with, and arranged meetings with, the employee to discuss matters, which the employee ignored.

Legal principle

The employee had been in repudiatory breach in wilfully failing to respond to the employer's correspondence and attend meetings. Such actions on the part of an employee undermined the trust and confidence inherent in the contract of employment and so the employee was in breach of duty.

Duty of fidelity, loyalty and confidentiality?

An employee is under an implied duty of fidelity and loyalty to his or her employer. Whether such a duty has been breached in a particular case will depend on the facts and circumstances. The effect of a breach by an employee is that an employer is

Figure 3.1

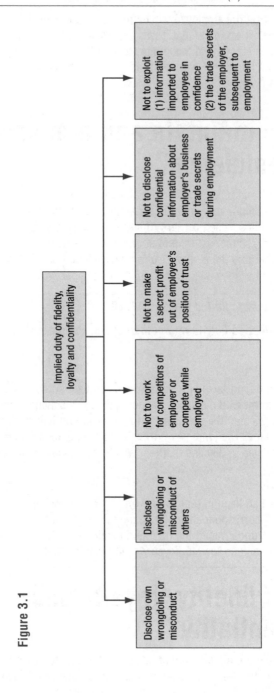

Implied duty of fidelity, loyalty and confidentiality

- Disclose own wrongdoing or misconduct

- Disclose wrongdoing or misconduct of others

- Not to work for competitors of employer or compete while employed

- Not to make a secret profit out of employee's position of trust

- Not to disclose confidential information about employer's business or trade secrets during employment

- Not to exploit (1) information imported to employee in confidence (2) the trade secrets of the employer, subsequent to employment

entitled to sue for an account of profits generated by the employee as a result of such breach.

Content and nature of the implied duty

The implied duty of fidelity, loyalty and confidentiality of the employee can be divided into six sub-duties. There is some overlap between each of them. See Figure 3.1.

Duty to disclose own wrongdoing

The cases of *Bell* v. *Lever Bros. Ltd* (1932) and *Sybron Corp.* v. *Rochem Ltd* (1983) established that an employee is not under an obligation to disclose their own wrongdoing or misdeeds to their employer. However, the position has altered recently – the case of *Item Software (UK) Ltd* v. *Fassihi* (2004) held that a senior employee who was also a director does owe such a duty to his or her employer. For a summary of the legal developments in this area, see Figure 3.2.

Figure 3.2

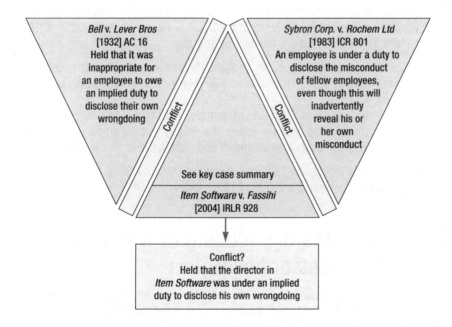

Bell v. *Lever Bros*
[1932] AC 16
Held that it was inappropriate for an employee to owe an implied duty to disclose their own wrongdoing

Conflict

Sybron Corp. v. *Rochem Ltd*
[1983] ICR 801
An employee is under a duty to disclose the misconduct of fellow employees, even though this will inadvertently reveal his or her own misconduct

Conflict

See key case summary

Item Software v. *Fassihi*
[2004] IRLR 928

Conflict?
Held that the director in *Item Software* was under an implied duty to disclose his own wrongdoing

Item Software (UK) Ltd v. *Fassihi* [2004] IRLR 928

Concerning: implied duty to disclose misconduct

Facts

This case concerned whether the duty of fidelity required a director to disclose important information known to him which was relevant to negotiations which he had been involved in on behalf of his employer. The director had sought to use that information to divert an important contract from his employer to a company which he owned.

Legal principle

The Court of Appeal held that as a matter of policy, a director, being a fiduciary, is under a duty to disclose his own wrongdoing or misconduct to his or her employer.

Problem area Disclosure: employees

The extent to which the duty to disclose wrongdoing applies to employees in general is not wholly clear from the judgments of the Court of Appeal in *Item Software (UK) Ltd* v. *Fassihi*. However, what does appear clear is that:

■ *Bell* v. *Lever Bros Ltd* (1932) is not an authority for the proposition that there are no circumstances in which an employee can have a duty to disclose his own wrongdoing; and
■ an employee who engages in illegal or fraudulent actions will be under such a duty to disclose, provided that they are acting as a fiduciary of the employer or where the employer has expressly imparted trust and confidence in that employee.

See Alan Berg (2005) 'Fiduciary Duties: A Director's Duty to Disclose His Own Misconduct', 121 *Law Quarterly Review* 213 for further reading.

Duty to disclose wrongdoing or misconduct of other employees or colleagues

Where an employee becomes aware of the misconduct or wrongdoing of other employees, they are under a duty to disclose such misconduct to their employer. See *Sybron Corp* v. *Rochem Ltd* (1983).

Duty not to work for competitors of the employer or compete with employer

An employee owes an implied obligation not to:

■ work for enterprises which compete with their employer; or
■ trade directly in competition with their employer.

The competing activities may take place during their own spare time or the working time of their employer.

Hivac v. *Park Royal Scientific Instruments* **[1946] Ch 169**

Concerning: implied duty not to work for competitors, breach

Facts

The employer manufactured valves. Their employees were extremely skilled in assembling those valves. On Sundays during their day off, the employees assembled valves for competitors of their employer.

Legal principle

The Court of Appeal held that the employees had breached the duty of good faith and fidelity, despite the fact that the work undertaken for the competitor was conducted in their own spare time.

Problem area When is an employee competing with the employer?

Where an employee intends to leave the employment of the employer for the purposes of setting up in competition with their employer and before or after so leaving does not disclose or exploit the confidential information or trade secrets of the employer, it is a matter of fact and degree whether an employee:

1. is actually competing with their employer; or
2. simply has the intention of setting up in competition with the employer in the future.

Situation 1 amounts to a breach of duty, whereas 2 does not. Which side of the divide between 1 and 2 the actions of the employee will fall is a matter of fact and degree. See Figure 3.3.

Figure 3.3

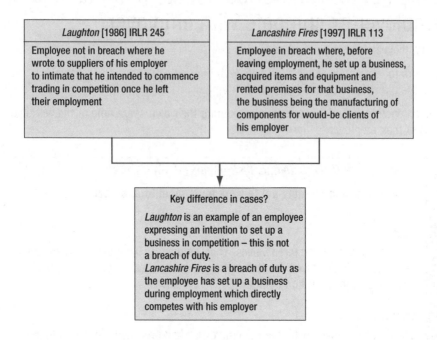

Problem area Competing after employment?

An employee is free to compete with his employer subsequent to the termination of his contract of employment. However, an express term called a restrictive covenant may be included in his contract of employment which prohibits him from competing with a competitor of his employer or setting up in competition with his employer after employment. The common law position is that such a 'non-compete' restrictive covenant is contrary to public policy and will be enforceable only so long as it is no wider than necessary to provide reasonable and adequate protection of the legitimate interests of the employer.

Duty not to make a secret profit

An employee is under an implied duty not to make a secret profit out of his or her position without the knowledge or consent of the employer. Where such a secret profit has been generated, the employee must account to the employer for it.

Confidential information and trade secrets: during employment

During the course of their employment, an employee is under an implied duty not to disclose or exploit confidential information about their employer's business or the trade secrets of their employer. An employer can seek an injunction or interdict to restrain the employee from making disclosure. However, during the course of their employment, an employee is entitled to disclose or exploit the general skill and knowledge which has been amassed during that period.

Problem area Effect of statutory law and human rights law

An employee's obligation not to disclose or exploit confidential information about the employer's business or the trade secrets of the employer is not absolute. Sections 43A–43M of the ERA 1996 offer protections to employees who release confidential information in relation to their employer's business to various parties where such disclosure is in the public interest. Furthermore, the implied duty not to disclose confidential information is subject to the employee's right to freedom of expression in Article 10 of the European Convention of Human Rights (incorporated by virtue of Sch. 1 to the Human Rights Act 1998).

Confidential information and trade secrets: after employment

There is a distinction between:

1. the general skill, know-how and knowledge which an employee has;
2. information about the employer's business which is in the public domain or has been learnt by the employee during the course of his employment;
3. information about the employer's business which has been imparted to the employee in confidence during the course of his employment; and
4. the trade secrets of the employer.

An employee is under a duty not to disclose or exploit 3 or 4 subsequent to the date of termination of their employment, whereas 1 and 2 are freely transferable. A clear example of 4 arises where an employee leaves employment to set up in competition with the employer and before doing so transfers files containing secret information to a USB key, taking it away with him and subsequently exploiting it.

Faccenda Chicken Ltd v. *Fowler* [1986] IRLR 69

Concerning: implied duty not to disclose trade secrets subsequent to date of termination of employment

Facts

The employer's business was the sale of fresh chickens. The employee was the sales manager. Thus, he was privy to customer lists, pricing policies and information regarding the quantity and quality of the goods sold. The employee left employment to set up in competition with his employer, selling the same products to the same clients.

Legal principle

The information used by the employee was not information about the employer's business which had been imparted to the employee in confidence during the course of his employment. Nor did it amount to the trade secrets of the employer. Accordingly, the employee was not in breach of the implied duty of fidelity. See Figure 3.4.

Restrictive covenants

It is open to an employer to include restrictive covenants in the contract of employment of the employee. These restrict the employee from disclosing *any* confidential information or trade secrets of the employer subsequent to employment. Such express terms complement the implied terms of the contract of employment, thus increasing the protection available to the employer. The common law position is that such restrictive covenants are contrary to public policy and will be enforceable only so long as they are no wider than necessary to provide reasonable and adequate protection of the legitimate interests of the employer.

Figure 3.4

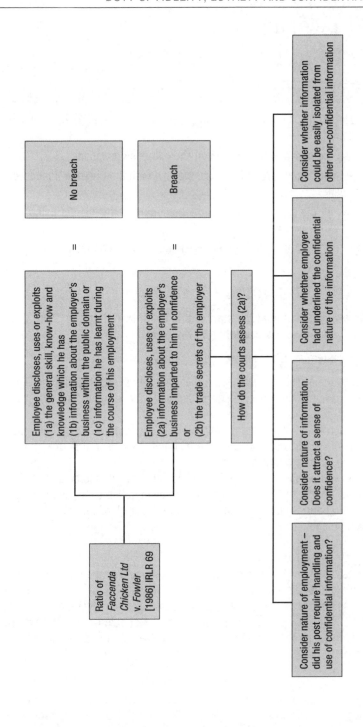

Ratio of *Faccenda Chicken Ltd v. Fowler* [1986] IRLR 69

Employee discloses, uses or exploits
(1a) the general skill, know-how and knowledge which he has
(1b) information about the employer's business within the public domain or
(1c) information he has learnt during the course of his employment

= No breach

Employee discloses, uses or exploits
(2a) information about the employer's business imparted to him in confidence
or
(2b) the trade secrets of the employer

= Breach

How do the courts assess (2a)?

Consider nature of employment – did his post require handling and use of confidential information?

Consider nature of information. Does it attract a sense of confidence?

Consider whether employer had underlined the confidential nature of the information

Consider whether information could be easily isolated from other non-confidential information

Chapter summary
Putting it all together

TEST YOURSELF

☐ Can you tick all the points from the revision checklist at the beginning of this chapter?

☐ Take the **end-of-chapter quiz** on the companion website.

☐ Test your knowledge of the cases below with the **revision flashcards** on the website.

☐ Attempt the essay question at the beginning of the chapter using the guidelines below.

☐ Go to the companion website to try out other questions.

Answer guidelines

See the essay question at the start of this chapter. A diagram illustrating how to structure your answer is available on the website.

Points to remember when answering this question:

▪ Refer to the implied duties having the common law as their source. The implied duties have been established, amended and refined by the courts over time on a case-by-case basis.

▪ Take each implied duty in turn and analyse and explain its content, nature and scope in a methodical manner. There should be a clear structure and a logical flow from one implied duty to the next.

▪ Finally, your essay should have a conclusion. This should clearly state that the content, scope, nature and quantity of implied duties continue to be developed by the courts and tribunals in light of statutory, social, economic and political developments.

Make your answer stand out

▪ Address the possible path and future development of the implied duties.

▪ Include a brief discussion of the extent to which statutory developments and express contractual provisions have affected or may affect the implied duties.

▪ The common law source of the implied duties should be commented upon and the extent to which this renders it unlikely that the list of implied duties could ever be closed.

4
Key statutory employment rights

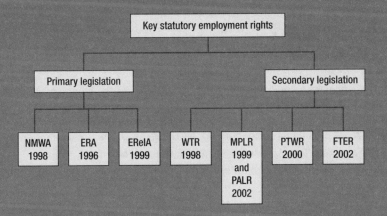

Revision Checklist

What you need to know:

☐ The key statutory rights of employees and workers under the Employment Rights Act 1996 and the Employment Relations Act 1999

☐ The rights of workers under the National Minimum Wage Act 1998

☐ Maternity, Paternity and Parental Leave rights in terms of the Employment Rights Act 1996, the Maternity and Parental Leave etc. Regulations 1999 and the Paternity and Adoption Leave Regulations 2002

☐ The rights of employees under subordinate legislation such as the Working Time Regulations 1998, the Part-Time Workers (Prevention of Less Favourable Treatment) Regulations 2000 and the Fixed-Term Employees (Prevention of Less Favourable Treatment) Regulations 2002.

Introduction:
Understanding key statutory employment rights

Employment protection legislation confers a number of statutory rights upon employees.

This chapter concentrates on a selection of the statutory rights of employees. The sources of these rights vary from primary legislation, such as the Employment Rights Act 1996 and the National Minimum Wage Act 1998, to secondary legislation, such as the Working Time Regulations 1998 and the Part-Time Workers (Prevention of Less Favourable Treatment) Regulations 2000. In recent years, a high proportion of secondary legislation conferring statutory employment rights has originated from the European Union.

Essay question advice

Essays require broad general knowledge of the main statutory rights of the employee. The examiner will also be looking for an examination of the main stimulus for the creation of some of the statutory rights, namely the EC. In addressing the broader aspects of the key statutory employment rights, the examiner will also expect you to address the proper method of enforcement of such statutory rights. In tackling essay questions, you should always directly answer the question(s) asked and apply the relevant law.

Where a problem question requires you to address key statutory employment rights, you will be required to demonstrate that you have identified and interpreted the relevant primary or secondary legislation in the correct manner. Moreover, you will be expected to take into account any potential exceptions and the appropriate means of enforcement of these rights. Where the source of a statutory employment right is EC law, the implications of this should also be considered. On this point, see Chapter 1. In tackling problem questions, you should always directly answer the question(s) asked and apply the relevant law to the facts at hand.

Sample question

Could you answer this question? Below is a typical problem question that could arise on this topic. Guidelines on answering the question are included at the end of the chapter, whilst a sample essay question and guidance on tackling it can be found on the companion website.

Problem question

Michael has been employed as a financial accountant for 15 years. He has worked an average of 57 hours per working week in the past calendar year. He is proposing to take action against his employer under the Working Time Regulations 1998. Advise Michael of his rights. Not long after visiting you, his employer dismisses him without notice and for no reason. Advise Michael.

■ Rights under the National Minimum Wage Act 1998

The National Minimum Wage Act 1998 contains two key protections in the context of the minimum wage. The national minimum wage is set by the Secretary of State annually by regulations.

KEY STATUTORY PROVISION

National Minimum Wage Act 1998 ('NMWA' 1998'"), s. 1(1)

A person who qualifies for the national minimum wage shall be remunerated by his employer in respect of his work in any pay reference period at a rate which is not less than the national minimum wage.

KEY STATUTORY PROVISION

NMWA 1998, s. 23(1)

A worker has the right not to be subjected to any detriment by any act, or any deliberate failure to act, by his employer, done on the ground that –

    (a) any action was taken, or was proposed to be taken, by or on behalf of the worker with a view to enforcing, or otherwise securing the benefit of, a right of the worker's. . .; or. . .

    . . .

    (c) the worker qualifies, or will or might qualify, for the national minimum wage or for a particular rate of national minimum wage.

Enforcement of NMWA 1998, ss. 1 and 23

Section 17 of the NMWA 1998 and the case of *Walton* v. *Independent Living Organisation Ltd* (2002) demonstrate that an employee's right under s. 1 of the NMWA 1998 is enforceable by raising an action for a breach of the terms of their contract of employment in the courts. Hence, although a statutory provision, s. 1 confers a contractual right upon an employee. Meanwhile, the appropriate method of enforcement of s. 23 of the NMWA 1998 is the presentation of a complaint to an employment tribunal in terms of s. 24 of the Act.

REVISION NOTE

The statutory right of a worker to be paid the national minimum wage should be taken into account when considering the implied duty of the employer to pay the employee wages even where there is no work. Provided the employee is ready and willing to work, payment will be due by the employer at the minimum wage.

■Rights under the Employment Rights Act 1996

The Employment Rights Act 1996 ('ERA 1996') contains a large number of statutory rights which are provided to employees. This chapter seeks to outline only some of them and the means by which they are enforced.

The right to receive a statement of the particulars of employment

An employee has a statutory right to receive certain information about their employment under s. 1(1) and (2) of ERA 1996. Sections 1(3), (4), (5), 2, 3 and 4 specify the 'particulars of employment' referred to in ERA 1996, s. 1(1) and (2). Section 11 of the Act provides that the rights in ERA 1996, s. 1(1) and (2) are to be enforced by making a complaint to an employment tribunal.

The right of an employee not to suffer unauthorised deductions from their wages

Subject to certain exceptions, the employer is prohibited from deducting sums from the wages of a worker.

<table>
<tr><td rowspan="5">KEY STATUTORY PROVISION</td><td>ERA 1996, s. 13(1)</td></tr>
<tr><td>An employer shall not make a deduction from wages of a worker employed by him unless –</td></tr>
<tr><td>(a) the deduction is required or authorised to be made by virtue of a statutory provision or a relevant provision of the worker's contract, or</td></tr>
<tr><td>(b) the worker has previously signified in writing his agreement or consent to the making of the deduction.</td></tr>
</table>

ERA 1996, s. 23(1) provides that the right in s. 13(1) of the Act is to be enforced by making a complaint to an employment tribunal.

The right of an employee not to suffer any detriment

ERA 1996, ss. 44, 45A, 47 and 47A–47E each provide that an employee is not to suffer any detriment at the hands of an employer for a number of reasons, including the following:

- a failure to obey the employer's orders for health and safety reasons;
- a refusal on the part of the employee to comply with a requirement imposed by the employer which is in contravention of the Working Time Regulations 1998; and
- the making of a protected disclosure by the employee.

In terms of ERA 1996, s. 48, each of the employee's rights under ERA 1996, ss. 44, 45A, 47 and 47A–47E are to be enforced by making a complaint to an employment tribunal.

The right to receive minimum periods of notice

If an employer proposes to terminate the employment of an employee, statute dictates that certain minimum periods of notice must be given by the former to the latter.

KEY STATUTORY PROVISION

ERA 1996, s. 86(1)

The notice required to be given by an employer to terminate the contract of employment of a person who has been continuously employed for one month or more –

(a) is not less than one week's notice if his period of continuous employment is less than two years,

(b) is not less than one week's notice for each year of continuous employment if his period of continuous employment is two years or more but less than twelve years, and

(c) is not less than twelve weeks' notice if his period of continuous employment is twelve years or more.

Where an employer fails to observe the terms of ERA 1996, s. 86(1), an employee is entitled to enforce this right by raising a court action for a breach of the terms of their contract of employment.

The right to be provided with a written statement of the reasons for dismissal

When an employee's employment is terminated by an employer with or without notice, the employer must provide the employee with a written statement of the reasons for their dismissal under ERA 1996, s. 92(1). The right in s. 92(1) is enforceable by making a complaint to an employment tribunal in terms of s. 93(1)(a) of the Act.

▮Rights under the Employment Relations Act 1999

Section 10 of the Employment Relations Act 1999 ('ERelA 1999') affords a key right to a worker. It enables a worker to be accompanied by a person at a disciplinary or grievance hearing. The worker's companion has the right to address the hearing, put forward the worker's case, sum up the case and respond on the worker's behalf to any view expressed at the hearing. Under s. 12 of the ERelA 1999, the worker has the right not to suffer any detriment or dismissal because he exercised such a right. The rights afforded to the worker under s. 10 of the ERelA 1999 are enforceable by raising a complaint in an employment tribunal by virtue of s. 11(1) of the Act.

▮Rights under the Working Time Regulations 1998

Rights are conferred on workers in terms of the Working Time Regulations 1998 ('WTR 1998'). We will concentrate on the four principal rights. The source of the rights in the WTR 1998 is EC Directive 93/104/EC of 23 November 1993 concerning certain aspects of the organisation of working time. For a summary of domestic legislation which is based on EC law, see Figure 4.1.

Figure 4.1

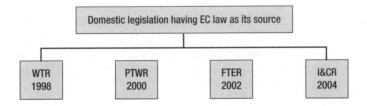

Maximum weekly working time

An employee has a statutory right not to be compelled to work in excess of an average of 48 hours in a working week.

KEY STATUTORY PROVISION

WTR 1998, reg. 4(1) and (2)

(1) Unless his employer has first obtained the worker's agreement in writing to perform such work a worker's time, including overtime, in any reference period which is applicable in his case shall not exceed an average of 48 hours for each seven days.

(2) An employer shall take all reasonable steps, in keeping with the need to protect the health and safety of workers, to ensure that the limit specified in paragraph (1) is complied with in the case of each worker employed by him in relation to whom it applies ...

Enforcement of WTR 1998, reg 4(1) and (2)

The key mechanism for the enforcement of reg. 4(1) of the WTR 1998 was explained in the case of *Barber* v. *RJB Mining (UK) Ltd* (1999). It confers a contractual right on an employee (and a corresponding contractual obligation on the employer) which is enforceable by a common law action. Meanwhile, a failure on the part of an employer to comply with reg. 4(2) of the WTR 1998 can be addressed by criminal sanction only. The right cannot be enforced by presenting a complaint to an employment tribunal. Moreover, *Sayers* v. *Cambridgeshire County Council* (2007) decided that a breach of reg. 4(2) of the WTR 1998 does not give rise to a cause of action for breach of statutory duty.

WTR 1998 opt-out

The importance of the words 'Unless his employer has first obtained the worker's agreement in writing to perform such work' in reg. 4(1) of the WTR 1998 cannot be overstated. These words enable an employer to opt out of the 48-hour weekly limit. This is achieved by obtaining the employee's consent in an agreement in writing.

'On-call' time

Regulation 2 of the WTR 1998 defines 'working time' as any period during which the employee is working, at his employer's disposal and carrying out his activity or duties. On this basis, does time spent by an employee on-call at or outside the workplace constitute working time?

SIMAP v. *Conselleria de Sanidad y Consumo de la Generalidad Valenciana* [2000] IRLR 845

Concerning: 'On-call' time, working time

Facts

A trade union for doctors in Spain ('SIMAP') raised a claim against the Ministry of Health for the Valencia Region in Spain. They argued that 'working time' covered time spent on call by the doctors at a health centre.

Legal principle

The ECJ held that time spent on call by the doctors amounted to 'working time'. The key factor in this case was that the doctors were required to be present at a health centre when they were working on-call. Hence, where a worker spends time on-call, but is free to pursue their own leisure interests and does not require to be present or available at a particular workplace location, such time will not be included in determining 'working time'.

Daily rest and weekly rest

An employee has the right to daily rest and weekly rest breaks.

WTR 1998, regs 10(1) and 11(1)

10(1) A worker is entitled to a rest period of not less than eleven consecutive hours in each 24-hour period during which he works for his employer.

11(1) Subject to paragraph (2), a worker is entitled to an uninterrupted rest period of not less than 24 hours in each seven-day period during which he works for his employer.

The rights afforded to the worker under the WTR 1998, regs 10(1) and 11(1) can be enforced by raising a complaint in an employment tribunal by virtue of reg. 30(1)(a) of the WTR 1998.

Annual leave

Regulation 13(1) of the WTR 1998 provides an employee with the right to a minimum of four weeks' annual leave in a holiday year. It is enforceable by presenting a complaint to an employment tribunal.

Not to suffer a detriment under ERA 1996, s. 45A

Section 45A of the ERA 1996 complements the WTR 1998. It provides that a worker has the right not to be subjected to any detriment by any act, or any deliberate failure to act, by his employer on certain grounds, e.g. that the worker:

- refused to comply with an employer's instruction which contravened the WTR 1998;
- refused to give up a right conferred by the WTR 1998; or
- brought proceedings against the employer to enforce a right under the WTR 1998.

A worker can enforce the right under s. 45A of the ERA 1996 by presenting a complaint to an employment tribunal under s. 48(1ZA) of the Act.

■Maternity, paternity and parental leave rights

Maternity rights

Sections 71 and 73 of the ERA 1996 and regs. 4 and 7 of the Maternity and Parental Leave etc. Regulations 1999 ('MPLR 1999') provide an employee with the right to:

- 26 weeks' ordinary maternity leave ('OML'); and
- 26 weeks' additional maternity leave ('AML') from work.

During the periods of OML and AML, the employee continues to have the benefit of their terms and conditions of employment, with the exception of pay. In terms of s. 72 of the ERA 1996 and reg. 8 of the MPLR 1999, an employee has a right to compulsory maternity leave of two weeks which commences with the day on which childbirth occurs. If an employee is subjected to a detriment by her employer for reasons connected with maternity leave, she may present a complaint to an employment tribunal under s. 48 (1) of the ERA 1996.

Paternity rights

Provided an employee is able to satisfy:

■ that he is the father of a child or married to or the civil partner or partner of a child's mother; and
■ the other conditions in terms of reg. 4(2) of the Paternity and Adoption Leave Regulations 2002 ('PALR' 2002),

he is entitled to be absent from work on paternity leave in terms of reg. 4(2) of the PALR 2002 for the purpose of caring for a child or supporting the child's mother. An employee may take:

■ one week's paternity leave; or
■ two consecutive weeks' leave unpaid.

If an employee is subjected to a detriment by his employer for reasons connected with paternity leave, he may present a complaint to an employment tribunal under s. 48 (1) of the ERA 1996. Sections 3 and 4 of the Work and Families Act 2006 empower the Secretary of State to issue regulations increasing the period of paternity leave to 26 weeks.

Parental leave rights

If an employee is able to satisfy the relevant requirements and procedures in regs. 13 and 15 of, and Sch. 2 to, the MPLR 1999, he is entitled to be absent from work on unpaid parental leave for the purpose of caring for a child. The period of parental leave is fixed at a maximum of 13 weeks. An employee has no right to take more than four weeks' leave in any annual period. Section 80 of the ERA 1996 provides that an employee may present a complaint to an employment tribunal where the employer has prevented him or her or attempted to prevent him or her from taking parental leave.

■ Rights under the Part-Time Workers (Prevention of Less Favourable Treatment) Regulations 2000

In terms of reg. 5(1) of the Part-Time Workers (Prevention of Less Favourable Treatment) Regulations 2000 ('PTWR 2000'), a part-time worker has the right not to suffer:

■ less favourable treatment than a full-time worker (i.e. direct discrimination); or

■ a detriment, solely for the reason that he or she is a part-time worker.

The source of the rights in the PTWR 2000 is EC Directive 97/81/EC of 15 December 1997 concerning the Framework Agreement on part-time work. The right under reg. 5(1) of the PTWR 2000 applies only if the less favourable treatment is:

■ on the ground that the worker is a part-time worker; and
■ not justified on objective grounds.

In terms of reg. 8(1) of the PTWR 2000, any infringement of reg. 5 is enforceable by presenting a complaint to an employment tribunal.

KEY CASE

***Matthews* v. *Kent and Medway Towns Fire Authority* [2006] IRLR 367**

Concerning: reg. 5 of the PTWR 2000, appropriate comparator

Facts

Retained part-time fire-fighters argued that they were engaged in the same or broadly similar work as full-time fire-fighters working for the same employer. They also contended that both retained and full-time fire-fighters had the same type of contract described in terms of reg. 2(3)(a) of the PTWR 2000.

Legal principle

The House of Lords held that one had to look at the work that both the full-time worker and the part-time worker were engaged in and ask whether it was the same work or was broadly similar. Simply because the job of the full-time fire-fighter was a fuller, wider job than that of the retained fire-fighter was not the end of the exercise. One had to address the question posed by the statute, which was whether the work on which both groups were engaged could nevertheless be described as broadly similar. Accordingly, it was not open to the employment tribunal to conclude that the work of the full-time fire-fighter was not comparable with that of the retained fire-fighter.

Rights under the Fixed-Term Employees (Prevention of Less Favourable Treatment) Regulations 2002

The source of the rights in the Fixed-Term Employees (Prevention of Less Favourable Treatment) Regulations 2002 ('FTER 2000') is EC Directive 1999/70/EC of 28 June

1999 concerning the framework agreement on fixed-term work. Like the PTWR, reg. 3(1) of the FTER 2002 provides that a fixed-term employee has the right not to suffer:

■ less favourable treatment than a permanent employee (i.e. direct discrimination); or

■ a detriment, solely for the reason that he or she is a fixed-term employee.

The right under FTER 2002, reg. 3(3) applies only if the less favourable treatment is:

■ on the ground that the employee is a fixed-term employee; and

■ not justified on objective grounds.

Regulation 7(1) of FTER 2002 states that reg. 3 can be enforced by presenting a complaint to an employment tribunal.

Chapter summary
Putting it all together

TEST YOURSELF

☐ Can you tick all the points from the revision checklist at the beginning of this chapter?

☐ Take the **end-of-chapter quiz** on the companion website.

☐ Test your knowledge of the cases below with the **revision flashcards** on the website.

☐ Attempt the essay question at the beginning of the chapter using the guidelines below.

☐ Go to the companion website to try out other questions.

Answer guidelines

See the problem question at the start of this chapter. A diagram illustrating how to structure your answer is available on the website.

Points to remember when answering this question:

■ In your introduction, make the point that Michael has a number of heads of claim open to him.

■ You should consider whether Michael has a claim on the basis that his employer has breached reg. 4(1) and (2) of WTR 1998. How can Michael enforce this claim?

■ Address the issue of the statutory minimum periods of notice to which Michael is entitled and the effect of these entitlements.

■ Examine whether Michael has a statutory right to know why he has been dismissed.

Make your answer stand out

■ Analyse important case law which interprets the relevant piece of legislation, e.g. *Barber* v. *RJB Mining (UK) Ltd* (1999) and *Sayers* v. *Cambridgeshire County Council* (2007).

5
Discrimination in employment (1)

Revision Checklist

What you need to know:

☐ The definition of direct discrimination and how it is applied

☐ The definition of indirect discrimination and how it is applied

☐ An understanding of the concepts of harassment and sexual harassment

☐ An understanding of discrimination by way of victimisation

☐ An understanding of vicarious liability.

Introduction:
Understanding discrimination (1)

An employee has the statutory right not to be discriminated against on the grounds of their sex, race, disability, religious beliefs, philosophical beliefs, sexual orientation or age.

Anti-discrimination legislation is one of the key planks upon which the EU's and British Government's goal of achieving equality and diversity in the workplace is based. This chapter examines the principle of non-discrimination and examines the key components of such a principle as follows:

- direct discrimination;
- indirect discrimination;
- victimisation;
- harassment;
- sexual harassment; and
- vicarious liability of the employer for the discriminatory acts of its employees.

In Chapter 6, we will explore:

- the remedies available to an employee who has suffered discrimination;
- the exceptions to the non-discrimination principle;
- the burden of proof in discrimination cases; and
- aspects of age discrimination and **disability** discrimination in a greater amount of detail – since part of the disability and age discrimination regimes do not fully mirror the pattern established in the cases of sex, race, religious belief and sexual orientation discrimination legislation.

Essay question advice

Essays require broad general knowledge of the key concepts in anti-discrimination legislation, such as direct discrimination, indirect discrimination, victimisation, harassment, sexual harassment and vicarious liability. You should be able to explore each of these key concepts and to critically evaluate them. You should also be able to identify the elements of the key concepts which can be used as a defence by an employer. In tackling essay questions, you should always directly answer the question(s) asked and apply the relevant law.

Problem question advice

You may be given a set of facts relative to an individual employee and asked to advise that individual whether they have a reasonable prospect of success in presenting a complaint to an employment tribunal on the basis of the anti-discrimination legislation. Such a question seeks to identify your understanding of the key concepts in the legislation and how an employer may be able to raise a defence. In tackling problem questions, you should always directly answer the question(s) asked and apply the relevant law to the facts at hand. For example, if a problem question states that a female employee suffers from unwanted sexual advances from male colleagues, you should seek to ascertain whether the concept of sexual harassment in s. 4A(1)(b) of the Sex Discrimination Act 1975 is satisfied.

Sample question

Could you answer this question? Below is a typical essay question that could arise on this topic. Guidelines on answering the question are included at the end of the chapter, whilst a sample problem question and guidance on tackling it can be found on the companion website.

Essay question

Identify the four components of the test of indirect discrimination in the case of sex, race, religious belief, sexual orientation and age discrimination. Explain how each of these components might be used by an employer to defend an indirect discrimination claim.

■ The scope of discrimination law in the employment field

Anti-discrimination provisions cover the whole spectrum of the employment relationship, from selection and recruitment to promotion, transfer and dismissal.

KEY STATUTORY PROVISION

Sex Discrimination Act 1975 ('SDA 1975'), s. 6

(1) It is unlawful for a person, in relation to employment by him at an establishment in Great Britain, to discriminate against a woman –

    (a) in the arrangements he makes for the purpose of determining who should be offered that employment, or

    (b) in the terms on which he offers her that employment, or

    (c) by refusing or deliberately omitting to offer her that employment.

(2) It is unlawful for a person, in the case of a woman employed by him at an establishment in Great Britain, to discriminate against her –

    (a) in the way he affords her access to opportunities for promotion, transfer or training, or to any other benefits, facilities or services, or by refusing or deliberately omitting to afford her access to them, and

    (b) by dismissing her, or subjecting her to any other detriment.

In the case of racial discrimination, disability discrimination, religious discrimination, sexual orientation discrimination and age discrimination, respectively, similar provisions to those set out above are contained in the following:

- s. 4 of the Race Relations Act 1976 ('RRA 1976');
- s. 4 of the Disability Discrimination Act 1995 ('DDA 1995');
- reg. 6 of the Employment Equality (Religion or Belief) Regulations 2003, SI 2003/1660 ('EE(RB)R 2003');
- reg. 6 of the Employment Equality (Sexual Orientation) Regulations 2003, SI 2003/1660 ('EE(SO)R 2003'); and
- reg. 7 of the Employment Equality (Age) Regulations 2006, SI 2006/1031 ('EE(A)R 2006').

■ Definitions

The definitions which are relevant to an exam or problem question depend on which piece of anti-discrimination legislation you are being asked to consider.

SDA 1975, s. 82(1)

'woman' includes a female of any age.

RRA 1976, s. 3

(1) In this Act, unless the context otherwise requires –

'racial grounds' means any of the following grounds, namely colour, race, nationality or ethnic or national origins;

'racial group' means a group of persons defined by reference to colour, race, nationality or ethnic or national origins, and references to a person's racial group refer to any racial group into which he falls.

EE(RB)R 2003, reg. 2

(1) In these regulations –

(a) 'religion' means any religion,
(b) 'belief' means any religious or philosophical belief,
(c) a reference to religion includes a reference to lack of religion, and
(d) a reference to belief includes a reference to lack of belief.

REVISION NOTE

The definition of 'sexual orientation' is contained in reg. 2 of EE(SO)R 2003. The definition of disability in s.1 of the DDA 1995 will be considered separately in Chapter 6.

'Racial group'?

In *Mandla* v. *Dowell Lee* (1983), the House of Lords held that Sikhs were a 'racial group' within the meaning of s. 3 of the RRA 1976. Sikhs were a 'racial group' since they satisfied the following essential conditions:

■ they had a long shared history, distinguishing them from other groups;
■ they had a unique cultural tradition;
■ they had a common geographical origin or descent from a small number of common ancestors;
■ they had a common language;
■ they had a common literary heritage;

- they had a common religion distinguishing them from neighbouring groups; and
- they were a minority group.

Meanwhile, in *Dawkins* v. *Crown Suppliers* (1993) the Court of Appeal held that where there is no group language or descent and the group is essentially a religious sect, such as Rastafarians, s. 3 of the RRA 1976 will not have been satisfied.

'Religious or philosophical belief'?

Regulation 2(1) of the EE(RB)R 2003 originally defined 'religion or belief' as 'any religion, religious belief, or similar philosophical belief'. In *Baggs* v. *Fudge* (unreported) a BNP member claimed fascism was a 'similar philosophical belief'. However, it was held that the words 'similar philosophical belief' required that the philosophical belief be similar in nature to a religious belief. As a result, Baggs's claim was struck out. However, s. 77 of the Equality Act 2006 altered the definition of 'religion' and 'belief' in reg. 2(1) of the EE(RB)R 2003 in terms of the definition set out above. Accordingly, 'philosophical belief' is set apart from 'religion' or 'religious belief' and the word 'similar' has been removed. Therefore there is the possibility that *Baggs* might now be decided differently.

Problem area

The words 'religious or philosophical belief' appear to be wide enough to include groups such as Rastafarians within the compass of the protections in EE(RB)R 2003. Sometimes a group will enjoy protection under both the EE(RB)R 2003 and the RRA 1976 – e.g. Jews, who are undoubtedly a racial group for the purposes of s. 3 of the RRA 1976, but also a religion for the purposes of reg. 2 of the EE(RB)R 2003.

The prohibition of direct discrimination

The prohibition of direct discrimination is geared towards the eradication of unfavourable treatment of individuals forming part of a group in the workplace on the basis that they form part of that group. The legislation envisages persons being treated according to their merits, skills, qualities and defects.

KEY STATUTORY PROVISION

SDA 1975, s. 1(2)

(2) In any circumstances relevant for the purposes of a provision to which this subsection applies, a person discriminates against a woman if –

    (a) on the ground of her sex, he treats her less favourably than he treats or would treat a man . . .

Section 1(1) of the RRA 1976 and reg. 3 of the EE(RB)R 2003 and of the EE(SO)R 2003 are in similar terms.

REVISION NOTE

The test of direct disability discrimination follows the same patterns as direct sex, race, religious and sexual orientation discrimination. This will be considered in Chapter 6. However, the test of direct age discrimination in reg. 3(1) of the EE(A)R 2006 is unique and will be considered separately in Chapter 6.

Problem area Does the employer have a statutory defence to direct discrimination?

In the case of direct sex, race, disability, religion, belief and sexual orientation discrimination, the employer does not have a statutory defence. However, in the case of age, the proportionality defence is available to the employer in reg. 3 of the EE(A)R 2006. See Chapter 6.

'Less favourable treatment'

For the purposes of establishing 'less favourable treatment' and direct discrimination, a series of cases have decided that the motives, intention, policy reasons or criteria of an employer in discriminating are irrelevant. Originally, the courts took the view that whether there had been 'less favourable treatment' was primarily an issue of causation, i.e. a 'but for' test. The law has now changed. A 'reason why' test is now applied.

James v. *Eastleigh Borough Council* [1990] IRLR 288

Concerning: 'Less favourable treatment', 'but for' test

Facts

Mr and Mrs James were both aged 61. Mr James made a complaint that he had to pay to gain entrance to a council swimming pool whereas his wife did not. Entrance to the swimming pool was free for women aged 60 or over and men aged 65 or over.

Legal principle

The House of Lords held that Mr James had suffered direct discrimination. Building on its earlier jurisprudence in *R* v. *Birmingham County Council, ex p EOC* (1989), the House of Lords held that there was direct discrimination and less favourable treatment on the ground of sex if Mr James would have received the same treatment as females, but for his sex. Thus, a 'but for' test was applied.

Shamoon v. *RUC* [2003] IRLR 285

Concerning: 'Less favourable treatment', 'reason why' test

Facts

Shamoon was a chief inspector in the RUC. One of her functions concerned staff appraisals. A complaint was made against her by a Constable about the conduct of his appraisal. The complaint was upheld. A few months later, a complaint was made by another Constable about the terms of Shamoon's report on him. Responsibility for conducting appraisals was then removed from Shamoon. She claimed direct discrimination.

Legal principle

The House of Lords dismissed Shamoon's appeal for a number of reasons. Lord Nicholls held that it will sometimes be helpful to approach the question of direct discrimination by adopting a two-stage test:

■ first, to ask whether there was less favourable treatment; and
■ second, to ask whether it was on the grounds of sex.

In other words, one must ask 'the reason why' question after less favourable treatment has been proved to exist. However, Lord Nicholls cautioned against using the two-stage 'reason why' approach too rigidly. Sometimes (e.g. where the comparator is hypothetical), it will not be possible to decide whether there is less favourable treatment without deciding 'the reason why' first.

Figure 5.1

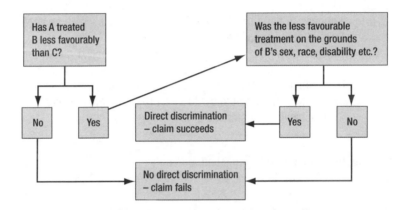

The requirement for a 'comparator'

Unlike the Equal Pay Act 1970, it is open to an employee to compare herself with a hypothetical comparator for the purposes of establishing whether there has been 'less favourable treatment'. This will be necessary where no actual comparator in the workplace can be identified. In selecting a fictitious comparator, a comparison of the cases must be such that the relevant circumstances in the one case are the same, or not materially different, in the other case – see SDA 1975, s. 5(3)(a).

■ The prohibition of indirect discrimination

The prohibition of indirect discrimination covers the situation where an employer applies a criterion or practice which by definition indirectly affects or prejudices certain groups of employees. The effect is called 'disparate impact'. There are four components to an indirect discrimination claim:

■ a provision, criterion or practice must have been applied;
■ particular group disadvantage must be established;

■ disadvantage to the claimant must be established; and
■ the employer must not be able to show that the application of the provision, criterion or practice was proportionate.

KEY STATUTORY PROVISION

SDA 1975, s. 1(2)

(2) In any circumstances relevant for the purposes of a provision to which this subsection applies, a person discriminates against a woman if –

. . .

(b) he applies to her a provision, criterion or practice which he applies or would apply equally to a man, but –
    (i) which puts or would put women at a particular disadvantage when compared with men,
    (ii) which puts her at that disadvantage, and
    (iii) which he cannot show to be a proportionate means of achieving a legitimate aim.

Similar definitions of indirect discrimination are contained in RRA 1976, s. 1(1A), EE(RB)R 2003, reg. 3(1)(b), EE(SO)R 2003, reg. 3(1)(b) and EE(A)R 2006, reg. 3(1).

REVISION NOTE

Please note that there is no such thing as indirect disability discrimination under the DDA 1995. However, an employer is under a duty to make reasonable adjustments where a provision, criterion or practice substantially disadvantages a disabled person. This is similar, albeit different, from the concept of indirect discrimination. See Chapter 6.

Dissecting the test of indirect discrimination

The test of indirect sex discrimination contained in the SDA 1975, s. 1(2) was implemented by the UK Government on 1 October 2005 by virtue of reg. 3 of the Employment Equality (Sex Discrimination) Regulations 2005. See Figure 5.2 which describes how an employee can satisfy an indirect discrimination claim.

Figure 5.2

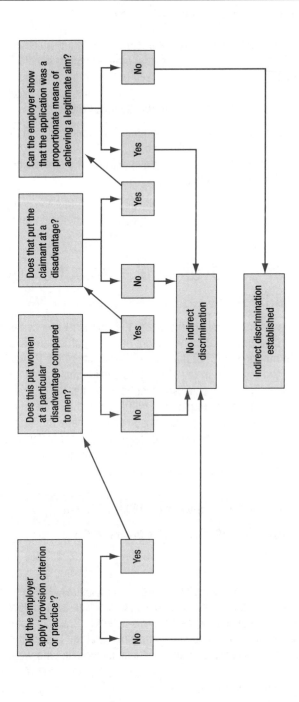

'Provision, criterion or practice'

These words replaced the words 'requirement or condition' which originally featured in the SDA 1975 and RRA 1976. The words 'requirement or condition' required the claimant to identify an absolute bar imposed by the employer upon compliance – *Perera* v. *Civil Service Commission (No. 2)* (1983). This was an exceptionally high hurdle for complainants to meet and so the law was relaxed:

- in 2001 (by the Sex Discrimination (Indirect Discrimination and Burden of Proof) Regulations 2001 (SI 2001/2660)); and
- again on 1 October 2005 (by the Employment Equality (Sex Discrimination) Regulations 2005 (SI 2005/2467)).

Hence, instead of being required to identify an absolute bar, the complainant is merely required to show a criterion, provision or practice which affects them.

'Particular disadvantage' – selection of a pool for comparison

In determining whether members (including the claimant) of a certain sex, race, religion, belief, sexual orientation or age are put at a 'particular disadvantage' when compared with others, s. 5(3) of the SDA 1975, s. 3(4) of the RRA 1976, reg. 3(3) of EE(RB)R 2003 and reg. 3(2) of EE(SO)R 2003 provide that a pool for comparison must be identified. The pools selected must be such that the relevant circumstances in one case are the same or not materially different in the other. In other words, a class of persons against whom a comparison can be made must be chosen in order to establish whether the complainant has been put at a particular disadvantage by the application of the provision, criterion or practice. Challenges to the suitability of one pool over others are a common feature of the cases.

KEY CASE

Jones v. University of Manchester [1993] IRLR 218

Concerning: suitability of 'pool' for comparison

Facts

The University advertised a post for a careers adviser. The person appointed required to be a graduate, preferably aged between 27 and 35 years of age. Ms Jones who applied for the post was aged 46. She was not shortlisted on the basis of her age and she complained that the University's requirements indirectly discriminated against women who were mature students.

▶

Legal principle

The Court of Appeal rejected Ms Jones's complaint. In the present case, Ms Jones's case was directed to proving:

■ not that the proportion of women graduates who could comply with the age requirement was considerably smaller than the proportion of men who could comply with it – as required by the statute,

■ but instead that the proportion of women mature graduates who could comply with the age requirement was considerably smaller – which is not what was required by the statute.

Problem area 'Particular disadvantage' – the role of statistics

Before the 2005 reforms, the complainant was required to show that a 'considerably smaller proportion' of the allegedly disadvantaged group could comply with the condition applied. This has been softened to the 'particular disadvantage' test which leaves a larger margin for error when statistics are considered. Thus, it is now the case that the scope for statistical discrepancies to defeat the complainant's case has been considerably reduced.

Proportionality – the employer's defence

The employer has a proportionality defence. In considering whether the employer's application of a provision, criterion or practice is a 'proportionate means of achieving a legitimate aim', the first thing is for the employer to identify their legitimate aim. It is then for the courts and tribunals to consider whether that aim is indeed 'legitimate'. If it is found to be legitimate, then the court and tribunal must ask whether the application of the provision, criterion or practice is a proportionate response to the achievement of that legitimate aim. It is inherent in the principle of proportionality that where different means of achieving a particular objective could be achieved, the one which has the least discriminatory impact should be chosen by the employer.

■ Harassment

There are now two forms of harassment prohibited under anti-discrimination legislation: first, there is harassment based 'on the grounds of' sex, race, disability, religion, belief, sexual orientation and/or age. Second, there is sexual harassment, which is essentially harassment of a sexual nature.

On the grounds of sex, race, disability, religion, belief, sexual orientation or age

KEY STATUTORY PROVISION

SDA 1975, s. 4A

(1) For the purposes of this Act, a person subjects a woman to harassment if –

    (a) on the ground of her sex, he engages in unwanted conduct that has the purpose or effect –
        (i) of violating her dignity, or
        (ii) of creating an intimidating, hostile, degrading, humiliating or offensive environment for her . . .

Section 3A of the RRA 1976, s. 3B of the DDA 1995, reg. 5 of the EE(RB)R 2003, reg. 5 of the EE(SO)R 2003 and reg. 6 of the EE(A)R 2006 are framed in similar terms.

Problem area Harassment 'on the grounds of'?

Article 2(2) of the Equal Treatment Directive 2002/73/EC (which applies to sex) defines harassment as 'where an unwanted conduct *related to* the sex of a person occurs with the purpose or effect of violating the dignity of a person, and of creating an intimidating, hostile, degrading, humiliating or offensive treatment'. Instead of using the words 'related to the sex', s. 4A of the SDA 1975 employs the words 'on the ground of her sex'. In the case of *R (EOC)* v. *Secretary of State for Trade and Industry* (2007), the High Court held that s. 4A does not adequately implement the Equal Treatment Directive. This was on the basis that the words 'on the ground of her sex' require the claimant to compare herself with a member of the opposite sex as a means of establishing harassment, whereas the words 'related to the sex' in the Equal Treatment Directive do not require such a comparison to be made. See Linda Clarke (2006) 'Harassment, Sexual Harassment, and the Employment Equality (Sex Discrimination) Regulations 2005', 35 *Industrial Law Journal* 161.

Sexual harassment

KEY STATUTORY PROVISION

SDA 1975, s. 4A

(1) For the purposes of this Act, a person subjects a woman to harassment if –

. . .

(b) he engages in any form of unwanted verbal, non-verbal or physical conduct of a sexual nature that has the purpose or effect –
(i) of violating her dignity, or
(ii) of creating an intimidating, hostile, degrading, humiliating or offensive environment for her . . .

Problem area 'Conduct of a sexual nature'?

The words 'conduct of a sexual nature' in s. 4A(1)(b) of the SDA 1975 are not defined. The Government had stated that ACAS would provide practical guidance as to what kind of conduct fell within these words. However, in their guidance paper entitled 'Bullying and Harassment at Work: A Guide for Managers and Employers' (2005), ACAS devolved responsibility for establishing instances of such conduct to employers themselves. However, what is clear is that a woman or man alleging sexual harassment on the basis of s. 4A(1)(b) of the SDA 1975 will not require to compare herself or himself with a member of the opposite sex. For further issues arising, see Linda Clarke (2006) 'Harassment, Sexual Harassment, and the Employment Equality (Sex Discrimination) Regulations 2005', 35 *Industrial Law Journal* 161.

EXAM TIP

You should be clear that you understand the difference between:

(a) harassment on the grounds of sex; and
(b) sexual harassment.

In a problem question, where the harassing conduct is sexual-neutral, but is directed at a particular gender, it is more likely that (a) above will be relevant. On the other hand, if the harassing conduct is of a sexual nature, e.g. offensive remarks, jokes or pictures, stalking or inappropriate physical contact, it is more likely that (b) is relevant.

▮Victimisation

B is victimised under s. 4 of the SDA 1975 where A treats B less favourably than A treats or would treat other persons and A does so by reason that:

(a) B has brought proceedings against A under the SDA 1975, the Equal Pay Act 1970 or the Pensions Act 1995;
(b) B has given evidence or information in connection with such proceedings;
(c) B has done anything under or by reference to the said Acts;
(d) B alleged that A or any other person has committed an act which would amount to a contravention of the said Acts; or
(e) A knows that B intends to do any of (a), (b), (c) or (d) or A suspects B has done, or intends to do any of them.

Section 2 of the RRA 1976, s. 55 of the DDA 1995, reg. 4 of the EE(RB)R 2003, reg. 4 of the EE(SO)R 2003 and reg. 4 of the EE(A)R 2006 are framed in similar terms.

EXAM TIP
In the context of problem questions, you should look out for facts which suggest that a worker is suffering some kind of detriment as a result of their gender, race, etc. Sometimes, the problem question will state that the victimisation or detriment has been threatened by the employer – you should be clear that such threats will also be covered within the statutory definition of victimisation.

▮Vicarious liability of employer for discriminatory acts of employees

Sections 41(1), 32(1) and 58(1) of the SDA 1975, RRA 1976 and DDA 1995, respectively, regs. 22(1) of each of the EE(RB)R 2003 and the EE(SO)R 2003 and reg. 25(1) of the EE(A)R 2006 provide that an employer will be statutorily vicariously liable for discriminatory acts or harassment engaged in by their employees where such acts are done in the course of their employee's employment (whether done with the employer's knowledge or approval or not). An employer has a defence where they can demonstrate that they took such steps as were reasonably practicable to prevent the employee from engaging in the discriminatory treatment. In such cases, the test of common law vicarious liability is irrelevant.

Chapter summary
Putting it all together

☐ Can you tick all the points from the revision checklist at the beginning of this chapter?

☐ Take the **end-of-chapter quiz** on the companion website.

☐ Test your knowledge of the cases below with the **revision flashcards** on the website.

☐ Attempt the essay question at the beginning of the chapter using the guidelines below.

☐ Go to the companion website to try out other questions.

Answer guidelines

See the essay question at the start of this chapter. A diagram illustrating how to structure your answer is available on the website.

Points to remember when answering this question:

▌ You should be able to demonstrate that you appreciate that the definition of indirect discrimination has changed twice since 2001.

▌ You must address the meaning of the phrase 'provision, criterion or practice'.

▌ How do the courts and tribunals assess whether a group is placed at a 'particular disadvantage'?

▌ An exploration of the employer's proportionality defence is paramount – how does this operate in practice?

Make your answer stand out

▌ You should be able to examine the differences between the current test of 'indirect discrimination' and the previous two tests of indirect discrimination, e.g. 'requirement or condition', 'considerably smaller proportion', etc.

▌ Does the application of the new test of indirect discrimination make it slightly easier for claimants to be successful?

6
Discrimination in employment (2)

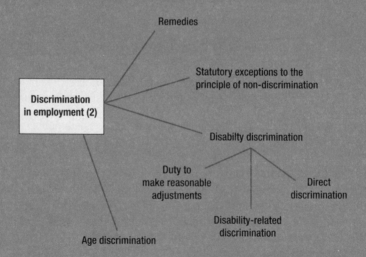

Remedies

Statutory exceptions to the principle of non-discrimination

Discrimination in employment (2)

Disabilty discrimination

Duty to make reasonable adjustments

Direct discrimination

Disability-related discrimination

Age discrimination

Revision Checklist

What you need to know:

☐ That there are statutory exceptions to the principle of non-discrimination

☐ The burden of proof in discrimination cases

☐ The meaning of 'disability-related discrimination'

☐ When an employer must make 'reasonable adjustments' in the context of a disability discrimination claim

☐ The key concepts contained in the age discrimination regulations.

Introduction:
Understanding discrimination (2)

The DDA 1995 prohibits disability-related discrimination and direct discrimination and imposes a duty to make reasonable adjustments

In this chapter, we will explore the remedies available to an employee who has succeeded in a discrimination claim and the exceptions to the principle of non-discrimination in the case of sex, race, religion, philosophical belief, sexual orientation or age, i.e. where it is lawful to discriminate against such groups. The burden of proof also requires to be considered. Finally, the concepts which are unique to the disability and age discrimination regimes will be examined.

Essay question advice

Essays require broad general knowledge of the remedies available to an employee pursuant to the anti-discrimination legislation and the exceptions to the anti-discrimination principle. An issue which is very topical is the burden of proof in discrimination cases. The burden of proof was altered in the case of sex discrimination and race discrimination relatively recently as a result of the introduction of ss. 63A and 66A of the Sex Discrimination Act 1975 and ss. 54A and 57ZA of the Race Relations Act 1976. Moreover, disability-related discrimination and the duty to make reasonable adjustments may be assessed and a firm grasp of how the courts and tribunals approach these issues is paramount. In tackling essay questions, you should always directly answer the question(s) asked and apply the relevant law.

Problem question advice

A problem question may require you to assess whether an employer has a defence to a sex, race, religion, etc. discrimination claim based on the application of one of the statutory exceptions in the relevant legislation. As for claims made under the DDA 1995, you may be asked to assess whether a claim based on the test of 'disability-related discrimination' or the employer's duty to make reasonable adjustments is likely to be successful or not. In tackling problem questions, you should always directly answer the question(s) asked and apply the relevant law to the facts at hand. For example, if a problem question provides that an employee in a wheelchair is unable to gain access to some part of their employer's premises, you should look to ascertain whether the employer's statutory duty to make reasonable adjustments in s. 3A(2) of the Disability Discrimination Act 1995 has been breached.

Sample question

Could you answer this question? Below is a typical problem question that could arise on this topic. Guidelines on answering the question are included at the end of the chapter, whilst a sample essay question and guidance on tackling it can be found on the companion website.

Problem question

Kashif Rao is a salesman working for a firm of computer software and hardware manufacturers. He is paid a very low basic salary of £8,000 per annum and the majority of his remuneration is made up of commission on sales, performance-related pay and bonuses. His job involves travelling by motor vehicle to clients of his employer located throughout the northern counties of England. After a minor road accident, he suffers from severe back pains when he drives a motor car for more than two hours at a time. His consultant's prognosis is that he suffers from a condition which is likely to have a long-term and substantial adverse effect on his ability to perform his duties since he is likely to suffer such severe back pains for the rest of his life. He is upset when his employer refuses to (i) provide him with additional breaks during his working day and (ii) modify his contractual remuneration structure. Advise Kashif.

▉ Remedies

The remedies available to an employee who has succeeded in their discrimination claim are as follows:

▪ an order declaring the rights of the employee and employer in relation to the act or acts to which the complaint relates;
▪ an order requiring the employer to pay compensation to the employee in the same manner in which damages in tort or reparation would be assessed in a court of law; or
▪ a recommendation that the employer take certain action within a specified period for the purpose of obviating or reducing the adverse effect of the discrimination.

The relevant provisions are contained in s. 65(1) of the Sex Discrimination Act 1975 ('SDA 1975'), s. 56(1) of the Race Relations Act 1976 ('RRA 1976'), s. 17A(2) of the Disability Discrimination Act 1995 ('DDA 1995'), reg. 30(1) of the Employment Equality (Religion or Belief) Regulations 2003, SI 2003/1660 ('EE(RB)R 2003'), reg. 30(1) of the Employment Equality (Sexual Orientation) Regulations 2003, SI 2003/1661 ('EE(SO)R 2003') and reg. 38(1) of the Employment Equality (Age) Regulations 2006, SI 2006/1031 ('EE(A)R 2006').

Calculation of compensation

In the majority of cases in which an employee is successful in their discrimination claim, compensation will be the remedy awarded by the employment tribunal. Unlike the remedy of compensation in the case of unfair dismissal, there is no cap on the amount of money which may be awarded to a successful employee. Indeed, awards of compensation can vary significantly. Where an employee or employer fails to follow the statutory disputes resolution procedures contained in Sch. 2 to the Employment Act 2002, the employment tribunal may reduce or increase the award of compensation by between 10% and 50%. A substantial percentage of the award will represent injury to the employee's feelings in suffering the discrimination, harassment or victimisation. In the case of *Vento* v. *Chief Constable of West Yorkshire Police (No. 2)* (2003), the Court of Appeal offered guidance on the range of awards for injury to feelings:

▪ awards of between £500 and £5,000 should be made for less serious cases, e.g. where the discrimination, harassment or victimisation is an isolated incident;
▪ awards of between £5,000 and £15,000 ought to be made for more serious cases, e.g. where there is a course of conduct amounting to discrimination, harassment or victimisation; and
▪ awards of between £15,000 and £30,000 should be made for the most serious cases where there has been a concerted crusade of discrimination, victimisation

and harassment. However, only in exceptional circumstances should the award for injury to feelings be more than £25,000.

■ 'Genuine occupational qualification' or 'genuine occupational requirement' exceptions

Anti-discrimination legislation pertaining to sex, race, religion, philosophical belief, sexual orientation and age contain certain provisions called 'genuine occupational qualifications' or 'genuine occupational requirements'. These provisions represent statutory exceptions to the general principle of non-discrimination. These exceptions are restricted to certain factual categories. For example, in the context of s. 7 of the SDA 1975 it is lawful to insist on a job being fulfilled by a man where this is required:

- for reasons of physiology (excluding physical strength or stamina);
- for reasons of authenticity, e.g. theatrical performers, actors and entertainers;
- for reasons of the preservation of decency or privacy; and/or
- in the context of a hospital, prison, residential care unit or nursing home.

Other genuine occupational requirements are contained in s. 7 of SDA 1975. With the exception of the disability discrimination legislation, each of the anti-discrimination regimes contains some form of genuine occupational qualification. However, each area is different and should be considered separately. See ss. 4A and 5 of the RRA 1976, reg. 7 of the EE(RB)R 2003, reg. 7 of the EE(SO)R 2003 and reg. 8 of the EE(A)R 2006.

EXAM TIP

In Chapter 5, you were introduced to the key concepts contained in anti-discrimination legislation such as direct discrimination, indirect discrimination, harassment and victimisation. A problem question may include facts which point towards a case of discrimination on one of these bases. However, the facts may concern someone employed (or seeking employment) as a theatrical performer, actor or in a prison, hospital or female nursing home (where there is scope for segregation of the sexes). Here, you should consider whether the genuine occupational qualifications exceptions may apply to defeat a complainant's discrimination claim.

■ Burden of proof

Once a complainant has established certain facts from which a tribunal could conclude that the employer has committed an act of discrimination or harassment, the onus of proof shifts to the employer to show that he has not committed such an act of discrimination or harassment.

KEY STATUTORY PROVISION

SDA 1975, s. 63A

(2) Where, on the hearing of the complaint, the complainant proves facts from which the tribunal could, apart from this section, conclude in the absence of an adequate explanation that the respondent –

    (a) has committed an act of discrimination or harassment against the complainant which is unlawful by virtue of Part 2 ... or

    (b) is by virtue of section 41 or 42 to be treated as having committed such an act of discrimination or harassment against the complainant,

the tribunal shall uphold the complaint unless the respondent proves that he did not commit, or, as the case may be, is not to be treated as having committed, that act.

Similar provisions apply in terms of s. 54A of the RRA 1976, reg. 29 of the EE(RB)R 2003, reg. 29 of the EE(SO)R 2003, s. 17A(1C) of the DDA 1995 and reg. 37 of the EE(A)R 2006.

Problem area

The application of the burden of proof test in practice has resulted in a great deal of litigation. See *Igen Ltd.*

KEY CASE

Igen Ltd v. *Wong* [2005] IRLR 258

Concerning: burden of proof, anti-discrimination legislation

Facts

This case considered whether the guidance of the EAT in *Barton* v. *Investec Henderson Crosthwaite Securities Ltd* (2003) ought to be applied or not.

Legal principle

The Court of Appeal held that the statutory provisions required an employment tribunal to apply the following two-stage process if a complaint were to be upheld:

▶

1. the complainant must prove facts from which the tribunal could conclude (in the absence of an adequate explanation from the employer) that the employer had committed, or was to be treated as having committed, the unlawful act of discrimination against the complainant; and

2. the second stage, which only comes into effect if the complainant has proved those facts, requires the employer to prove that he has not committed, or is not to be treated as having committed, the unlawful act. In order to do this, it is necessary for the employer to prove, on the balance of probabilities, that the treatment was in no sense whatsoever on a prohibited ground, i.e. sex, race, etc.

At the first stage, the tribunal must assume that the employer has advanced no adequate explanation for the primary facts proved by the complainant. At the second stage, the burden of proof has clearly shifted to the employer to the effect that they must provide an adequate explanation.

Further guidance on stages 1 and 2

Igen Ltd v. *Wong* established the two-stage test. However, some questions remained unanswered and have been subsequently resolved in respect of stage 1:

▌ In *Laing* v. *Manchester City Council* (2006), the EAT held that at stage 1, an employment tribunal is entitled to take into account all material facts (which can be distinguished from an adequate explanation advanced by the employer) in coming to a view.

▌ In *Brown* v. *London Borough of Croydon* (2007), where the claimant is comparing herself against a hypothetical comparator, the Court of Appeal held that it is good practice to apply the two-stage test, but that it is not an error of law for a tribunal to move straight to stage 2 without considering stage 1. Such an approach does not prejudice the employee.

▌ In *Madarassy* v. *Nomura International plc* (2007), the Court of Appeal held that in order to satisfy stage 1, an employee must show more than:

  ▌ a mere difference in sex between herself and the comparator (real or hypothetical); and

  ▌ a mere difference of treatment between herself and the comparator (real or hypothetical).

Hence, (a) a difference in sex + (b) a difference in treatment does not necessarily = the satisfaction of stage 1. All that (a) + (b) demonstrates is a possibility of discrimination and more evidence is required from the employee.

REVISION NOTE

The cases dealing with the burden of proof are very important for the purposes of the test of direct discrimination. If you compare the two-stage 'reason why' approach applied in the context of direct discrimination (see Chapter 5), it becomes clear that it mirrors the two-stage test in the case of the burden of proof. In other words, at stage 1, the onus lies on the employee to prove that the employee has suffered less favourable treatment or was to be treated as having suffered less favourable treatment. Thereafter, at stage 2, the burden shifts to the employer to prove that the 'reason why' was in no sense whatsoever to do with the employee's sex, race, disability, etc., i.e. a genuine non-discriminatory reason.

■ Disability discrimination

Disability

The definition of 'disability' is contained in s. 1 of the DDA 1995.

DDA 1995, s. 1

1(1) Subject to the provisions of Schedule 1, a person has a disability for the purposes of this Act if he has a physical or mental impairment which has a substantial and long-term adverse effect on his ability to carry out normal day-to-day activities.

See Figure 6.1 for the key components of 'disability'. 'Normal day-to-day activities' are defined in Sch. 1 to the DDA 1995 and some of the things covered are:

■ mobility;
■ manual dexterity;
■ physical co-ordination; and
■ continence.

Figure 6.1

Key component No.	Nature of key component
1	'Mental impairment' or 'physical impairment';
2	which has a 'substantial adverse effect', on 'normal day-to-day activities'; and
3	'long-term adverse effect' on 'normal day-to-day activities'

Disability: further guidance

Schedule 1 to the DDA 1995 provides further guidance as to what constitutes a 'disability'. For example, the words 'long-term effects', 'normal day-to-day activities' and 'substantial adverse effects' are defined and persons with cancer, HIV, MS and other prescribed conditions are deemed to be 'disabled'. Since 1 May 2006, the definitions of 'mental impairment' and 'physical impairment' in the DDA 1995 have been complemented by guidance issued by the Secretary of State for Work and Pensions (available from http://www.drc-gb.org/docs/DefnOfDisability.doc). An important point is that s. 18 of the DDA 2005 amended para. 1 of Sch. 1 to the DDA 1995 so that it is no longer necessary to show that an employee is suffering from a well-recognised mental illness for that person to be suffering from a 'mental impairment'.

Must the employer be aware of the disability?

If an employer has no knowledge of an employee's disability, do they have a valid defence to a claim based on the DDA 1995?

▮ In the case of a claim based on 'direct discrimination', the answer is probably not. Paragraph 4.11 of the Disability Rights Commission's ('DRC') Code of Practice in Employment and Occupation ('COP') provides that 'direct discrimination may sometimes occur even though the employer is unaware of a person's disability' (available from http://www.drc-gb.org/docs/2008_323_Employment_ Occupation.doc). Although not possessing the force of law, the COP can be used in evidence in an employment tribunal and the tribunals and courts must have regard to it.

▮ In the case of a claim based on 'disability-related discrimination', in *Taylor* v. *OCS Group Ltd* (2006), the Court of Appeal held that it is necessary to show that the fact that the individual was disabled was present in the employer's mind and that it had at least a significant influence on their decision.

▮ Meanwhile, in the case of the 'duty to make reasonable adjustments', an employer cannot be liable unless they knew, or ought reasonably to have known, that the disabled person had a disability and was likely to be put at a substantial disadvantage – see DDA 1995, s. 4A(3) and *Lanarkshire Primary Care NHS Trust* v. *Naicker* (UKEAT/0003/05, 18 May 2005).

Types of disability discrimination

Apart from harassment and victimisation on the grounds of disability (both considered in Chapter 5), there are essentially three key forms of disability discrimination:

(a) The duty to make reasonable adjustments;
(b) Disability-related discrimination; and
(c) Direct disability discrimination (considered in Chapter 5).

Some points on the interaction of (a), (b) and (c) are as follows:

▮ (b) above can be justified by the employer, but the employer's justification defence should not be considered by a tribunal unless the employer has satisfied (a) – *Archibald* v. *Fife Council* [2004] IRLR 651 at pp. 655–656 per Lord Rodger, and DDA 1995, s. 3A(6);
▮ an employer can justify (b), but such justification will not be possible if the relevant treatment amounts to (c) – see s. 3A(4) of the DDA 1995;
▮ (a) and (c) can never be justified by an employer; and
▮ (b) and (c) both involve the making of comparisons, but the comparisons are significantly different. In the case of (b), the comparison must be made with a person to whom the disability-related reason does not or would not apply – *Clark* v. *TDG Ltd t/a Novacold* (1999). For the purposes of (c), the comparator (actual or hypothetical), must not be disabled and must have the same (or not materially different) relevant circumstances as the disabled person.

Duty to make reasonable adjustments

The employer's duty to make reasonable adjustments is contained in s. 3A(2) of the DDA 1995.

DDA 1995, ss. 3A(2) and 4A(1)

3A(2) [a] person also discriminates against a disabled person if he fails to comply with a duty to make reasonable adjustments imposed on him in relation to the disabled person ...

4A(1) Where –

(a) a provision, criterion or practice applied by or on behalf of an employer, or

(b) any physical feature of premises occupied by the employer,

places the disabled person concerned at a substantial disadvantage in comparison with persons who are not disabled, it is the duty of the employer to take such steps as it is reasonable, in all the circumstances of the case, for him to have to take in order to prevent the provision, criterion or practice, or feature, having that effect.

Section 18B provides further guidance on the factors which a tribunal is required to consider in coming to a view as to whether a particular step would have been reasonable for an employer to take.

Archibald v. *Fife Council* [2004] IRLR 651

Concerning: duty to make reasonable adjustments

Facts

Mrs Archibald was employed as a road sweeper. After a routine surgical procedure she became unable to walk. This meant she could no longer do her job. Mrs Archibald applied for a number of sedentary office-based jobs. However, she was unsuccessful and was dismissed.

Legal principle

The House of Lords held that:

■ the DDA 1995 imposes a positive duty to make reasonable adjustments. Unlike the SDA 1975 and the RRA 1976, the DDA 1995 obliges an employer to positively discriminate in favour of disabled people, i.e. treat them differently – and more favourably – than non-disabled employees where the former have been put at a 'substantial disadvantage';

■ the positive obligation to make reasonable adjustments potentially includes:
  – allowing disabled people to trump applicants for existing vacancies even where the disabled person is not the best candidate for that vacancy, provided that the disabled person is suitable to do that work; and
  – creating a new post for the disabled employee.

Problem area In connection with what must 'reasonable adjustments' be made?

In *Nottinghamshire CC* v. *Meikle* (2004), the Court of Appeal made it clear that the duty to make reasonable adjustments extended beyond physical features of the workplace to terms, conditions and arrangements of the workplace such as hours of work, duties, contractual sick pay, etc. This is now reflected in ss. 4A(1) and 18B of the DDA 1995 which require the tribunal to consider whether:

(a) any provisions, criteria or practices, or
(b) physical features of the employer's premises,

put disabled persons at a 'substantial disadvantage' compared to non-disabled persons.

Requirement for a comparator

In determining whether there is a 'substantial disadvantage', a comparator for the disabled person must be selected. *Smith* v. *Churchills Stairlifts plc* (2006) held that the correct comparator is not the population as a whole, but those others who fulfil the other conditions for the job.

The 'reasonableness' test in ss. 3A(2) and 4A(1), DDA 1995

Two important points can be made in relation to the reasonableness test in ss. 3A(2) and 4A(1):

1. The 'reasonableness' test in ss. 3A(2) and 4A(1) is objective. This is amply demonstrated by *Collins* v. *Royal National Theatre Board Ltd* (2004) and the judgment of Kay LJ in *Smith* v. *Churchills Stairlifts plc* [2006] IRLR 41 at p. 47.
2. In considering the employer's duty to make reasonable adjustments in a given case, an employer will not be in breach of duty if they merely fail to consider making a proper assessment of the reasonable steps which they ought to take. Instead, the duty to make reasonable adjustments is limited to what an employer did or did not do – not what they had considered – see *Tarbuck* v. *Sainsbury's Supermarkets Ltd* (2006).

Disability-related discrimination

Disability-related discrimination is a concept which is peculiar to disability. It has no equivalent counterpart in other anti-discrimination legislation.

KEY STATUTORY PROVISION

DDA 1995, s. 3A(1) and (3)

3A(1) [a] person also discriminates against a disabled person if –

(a) for a reason which relates to the disabled person's disability, he treats him less favourably than he treats or would treat others to whom that reason does not or would not apply, and

(b) he cannot show that the treatment in question is justified.

. . .

(3) Treatment is justified for the purposes of subsection (1)(b) if, but only if, the reason for it is both material to the circumstances of the particular case and substantial.

Less favourable treatment

Disability-related discrimination is demonstrated for the purposes of s. 3A(1) if a disabled person is treated less favourably than a person to whom the disability-related reason does not or would not apply – *Clark* v. *TDG Ltd t/a Novacold* (1999). Hence the comparison focuses on the non-disability reason, rather than the disability itself. At para. 4.30 of the DRC's COP, the following useful example is given:

A disabled woman is refused an administrative job because she cannot type. She cannot type because she has arthritis. A non-disabled person who was unable to type would also have been turned down. The disability-related reason for the less favourable treatment is the woman's inability to type, and the correct comparator is a person to whom that reason does not apply – that is, someone who can type. Such a person would not have been refused the job. Nevertheless, the disabled woman has been treated less favourably for a disability-related reason and this will be unlawful unless it can be justified. There is no direct discrimination, however, because the comparator for direct discrimination is a person who does not have arthritis, but who is also unable to type.

Section 3A(1) justification: 'material and substantial'

An employer can justify disability-related discrimination. The justification must be 'both material to the circumstances of the particular case and substantial'. In *Jones* v. *Post Office* (2001), the Court of Appeal held that a tribunal should consider whether the reason advanced by the employer for the treatment of the disabled person fell within or outside the range of what a reasonable employer would have relied on as a material and substantial reason for the less favourable treatment. In other words:

■ a tribunal is not entitled to ask whether the employer's reason for the disability-related discrimination was material and substantial and then substitute its own judgment for that of the employer if it disagrees with the judgment of the employer; but

■ instead, the tribunal must consider whether the employer's reason fell within or outside the range of reasonable responses which the reasonable employer would have relied on as a material and substantial reason for the less favourable treatment.

REVISION NOTE

Comparing the 'justification' of disability-related discrimination with the 'duty to make reasonable adjustments'. The test for the justification of disability-related discrimination is subjective and operates like the 'range of reasonable responses' test in the context of unfair dismissal (see Chapter 9). The test for justification is in stark contrast to the nature of the employer's duty to make reasonable adjustments – which is objective. In other words, in the case of the duty to make reasonable adjustments, the tribunal must look at all the circumstances of the case in coming to a view as to whether the employer has met the duty to make reasonable adjustments and is perfectly entitled to substitute its own judgment for that of the employer.

FURTHER THINKING

Read the judgment of Mr Elias J in *Heathrow Express Operating Co. Ltd* v. *Jenkins* [2007] All ER (D) 144 (Feb) at paras 40–41. Note the differences in the tests for:

■ the justification of disability-related discrimination in s. 3A(1)(b) of the DDA 1995 (which is determined by the application of a subjective test); and
■ the duty to make reasonable adjustments in ss. 3A(2) and 4A of the DDA 1995 (which is determined by the application of an objective test)?

Do you agree with Mr Elias J's tentative justification for the differences in the above two tests?

Direct discrimination

The definition of direct discrimination is contained in s. 3A(5) of the DDA 1995.

KEY STATUTORY PROVISION

DDA 1995, s. 3A(5)

(5) A person directly discriminates against a disabled person if, on the ground of the disabled person's disability, he treats the disabled person less favourably than he treats or would treat a person not having that particular disability whose relevant circumstances, including his disabilities, are the same as, or not materially different from, those of the disabled person.

REVISION NOTE

Direct discrimination was examined in detail in Chapter 5. Direct disability discrimination follows the same pattern. See Figure 5.1 for an outline.

■Age discrimination

Age discrimination has been prohibited with effect from 1 October 2006 in terms of the Employment Equality (Age) Regulations 2006 ('EE(A)R 2006'). The EE(A)R 2006 follow the same pattern as other anti-discrimination legislation. However, there are some concepts which are specific to age discrimination which we will now consider.

Direct discrimination

Regulation 3(1) of the EE(A)R 2006 makes it clear that direct age discrimination may be justified by the employer if they can show that the less favourable treatment was a proportionate means of achieving a legitimate aim.

Figure 6.2

Legitimate aims
1 Protection or promotion of vocational integration of a particular age group
2 Fixing of a minimum age to recruit or retain older people
3 Health, welfare and safety
4 Particular training requirements
5 Recruiting or retaining older people
6 Encouraging and rewarding loyalty
7 The need for a reasonable period of employment before retirement

Figure 6.3

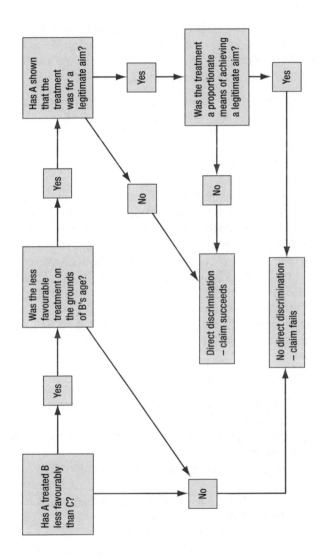

Problem area 'Less favourable treatment a proportionate means of achieving a legitimate aim'?

Both of the following documents provide guidance on what is meant by the words 'legitimate aim':

- Article 6.1 of the EC Framework Directive (2000/78/EC of 27 November 2000) – which the EE(A)R 2006 were introduced to partly implement; and
- Paragraph 4.1.17 of the DTI's Consultation Paper, *Equality and Diversity: Coming of Age* (available from http://www.dti.gov.uk/files/file16397.pdf)

'Legitimate aims' of the employer are listed in Figure 6.2. An adjusted flowchart for direct discrimination in the case of age is shown as Figure 6.3.

Retirement dismissals

If an employer forces an employee to retire, the retirement of that employee will amount to a 'dismissal' in terms of reg. 7(2)(d) of the EE(A)R 2006. On the face of it, this amounts to age discrimination and an unfair dismissal in terms of Part X of the Employment Rights Act 1996. However, forcing an employee to retire at the 'default retirement age' will not amount to unfair dismissal only if an employer follows the procedures in Sch. 6 to the EE(A)R 2006. Regulation 30 of the EE(A)R 2006 sets the default retirement age at 65. The Government has promised to re-consider the suitability of the default retirement age in 2011.

If an employer wishes to force an employee to retire at 65, Sch. 6 to the EE(A)R 2006 must be complied with. The basic elements of this procedure are shown in the Table opposite.

An employee will be unfairly dismissed if:

- the employee can show that the reason for their dismissal is not retirement on the planned date of retirement;
- the employer contemplated dismissing the employee for another reason in the preceding six months;
- the employer fails to notify the employee of their right to apply to continue working; or
- the employer dismisses the employee before a meeting to discuss the employee's request to continue working.

Date	Event
12 months before the intended date of retirement	Earliest date on which employer who intends to retire an employee must notify the employee of (i) the planned retirement date for that employee and (ii) the employee's right to make a request to the employer to continue working beyond the intended retirement date.
6 months before the intended date of retirement	(1) Last date on which employer who intends to retire an employee must notify the employee of (i) the planned retirement date for that employee and (ii) the employee's right to make a request to the employer to continue working beyond the intended retirement date without suffering fine of up to 8 weeks' wages #; and (2) earliest date for the notified employee to make a request to continue working beyond the planned retirement date.
3 months before the intended date of retirement	Last date for a notified employee to make a request to continue working if the employer gave notice between the 6-month and 12-month period before the intended date of retirement.
14 days before the date of dismissal	If the employer has not issued the employee with the date of the intended retirement by this date, any dismissal for retirement is an automatically unfair dismissal.
Intended date of retirement/dismissal	On this date (a) the employee will be dismissed or (b) the employee's date of retirement will be altered if the employee's request to continue working beyond the intended retirement date is granted by the employer.
Three months after the date # above or the date on which the employee knew that date	This is the deadline for the employee to present a complaint to an employment tribunal in respect of the employer's failure to notify the employee of (i) the planned retirement date for that employee and (ii) the employee's right to make a request to the employer to continue working beyond the intended retirement date.

Source: Adapted from: Sprack, J. (2006) Guide to the Age Discrimination Regulations 2006. Haywards Heath: Tottel Publishing.

The consolidation of all anti-discrimination legislation into one single Equality statute which includes the equal pay regime is currently being considered by the UK Government. The Discrimination Law Review, published on 12 June 2007, recommended the introduction of a single Equality Act. Do you agree that there is a need for a single Act?

■ The Equalities Review (2007) 'Fairness and Freedom: The Final Report of the Equalities Review', 28 February, pp. 115–116.
■ The Discrimination Law Review (2007) 'A Framework for Fairness: Proposals for a Single Equality Bill for Great Britain – A Consultation Paper', 12 June 2007.

Chapter summary
Putting it all together

☐ Can you tick all the points from the revision checklist at the beginning of this chapter?

☐ Take the **end-of-chapter quiz** on the companion website.

☐ Test your knowledge of the cases below with the **revision flashcards** on the website.

☐ Attempt the essay question at the beginning of the chapter using the guidelines below.

☐ Go to the companion website to try out other questions.

Answer guidelines

See the problem question at the start of this chapter. A diagram illustrating how to structure your answer is available on the website.

Points to remember when answering this question:

■ Explain that the employee may have a claim for breach of the employer's statutory duty to make reasonable adjustments.
■ Consider whether the employer has applied a 'provision, criterion or practice'.
■ If so, is the employee placed at a 'substantial disadvantage'? How do the tribunals ascertain whether there is 'substantial disadvantage'?
■ Examine the reasonable steps or adjustments which the employer might take in the employee's case.

Make your answer stand out

■ Consider the implications of *Archibald* v. *Fife Council*. Is it satisfactory that the duty to make reasonable adjustments involves employers positively discriminating in favour of disabled persons?

7
Equal pay

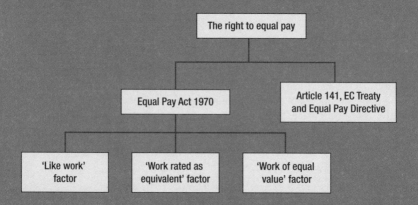

Revision Checklist

What you need to know:

- [ ] The content of the equality clause
- [ ] The distinction between the three criteria of 'like work', 'work rated as equivalent' and 'work of equal value' in s. 1 of the Equal Pay Act 1970 ('EPA 1970')
- [ ] The content of the employer's defence to an equal pay claim based on genuine material factors
- [ ] The relationship between the EPA 1970 and Article 141 of the EC Treaty.

Introduction:
Understanding equal pay

A female employee is entitled to the same pay as a suitable male employee comparator.

This chapter examines the principle of equal pay for equal work. It examines how a female employee is entitled to the same remuneration as a suitable male employee comparator. The equal pay rules are contained in s. 1 of the EPA 1970 and their intention is to eliminate sex discrimination in pay – not to secure 'fair wages'. In terms of s. 1(3) of the EPA 1970, an employer has a defence to an equal pay claim. Article 141 of the EU Treaty – which secures equal pay for equal work – must also be considered.

Essay question advice

Essays require broad general knowledge of the principles of equal pay in EPA 1970 and the exceptions to these principles. Essays may also require you to explore the right of an employee to equal pay under Article 141 of the EC Treaty and how the rules for establishing an equal pay claim differ under the UK and EC regimes. The means of enforcement of equal pay rights under EPA 1970 and Article 141 of the EC Treaty should be examined, compared and contrasted where this is necessary to answer the essay question. In tackling essay questions, you should always directly answer the question(s) asked and apply the relevant law.

Problem question advice

Most problem questions will involve an examination of the three differing equal pay criteria under s. 1 of the EPA 1970. In answering a problem question, candidates may be required to explore whether an employer will have the benefit of the genuine material factor defence. In order to appreciate when this exception/defence applies, candidates must fully understand the content of this defence and the circumstances in which the courts have held a factor to qualify as a genuine material factor. Problem questions may also steer the candidate towards a discussion of Article 141 of the EC Treaty. In tackling problem questions, you should always directly answer the question(s) asked and apply the relevant law to the facts at hand.

Sample question

Could you answer this question? Below is a typical essay question that could arise on this topic. Guidelines on answering the question are included at the end of the chapter, whilst a sample problem question and guidance on tackling it can be found on the companion website.

Essay question

Critically evaluate the 'genuine material difference/factor' defence which is open to an employer in terms of s. 1(3) of the EPA 1970. Do you believe the legal position is satisfactory?

■The equality clause

Section 1(1) of the EPA 1970 imposes an equality clause into the contract of employment of every individual employee. There are three principal components of the equality clause.

KEY STATUTORY PROVISION

EPA 1970, s. 1(1)

If the terms of a contract under which a woman is employed at an establishment in Great Britain do not include (directly or by reference to a collective agreement or otherwise) an equality clause they shall be deemed to include one.

Problem area Nature of the equality clause

One must be clear that s. 1(1) of the EPA 1970 imposes a contractual term into an employee's contract of employment. Since it is a contractual term, it can be enforced in the courts if it is breached. Section 2 of the EPA 1970 also provides for enforcement in the employment tribunals.

Pay

The EPA 1970 specifically prohibits discrimination in 'pay', i.e. pay-related contractual terms. Since a female employee's pay-related terms are compared with the same pay-related contractual terms of a male employee, sums payable under a contract such as bonuses, pension contributions and holiday entitlement are all covered and compared, term by term. If there is a valid equal pay claim, the pay-related terms of the female must be brought up into line with the same pay-related terms of the male. This is the case, irrespective of whether some of the other pay-related contractual terms of the female are better than those of the male. The word 'pay' has an even broader scope under Article 141 of the EC Treaty – see *Defrenne* v. *Belgium* [1971] ECR 445 (at p. 541).

EXAM TIP

In an essay question or problem question, look out for any assertion in the question that the employee is entitled to be paid a bonus. You should also look out for any suggestion of an employee receiving pension entitlements or contributions or enhanced redundancy benefits or long-term sickness benefits. These items are covered within the compass of EPA 1970 and the word 'pay' in Article 141 of the EC Treaty.

Do the female or male comparators require to work for the same employer?

The answer is no. Section 1(6) of the EPA 1970 provides that a man and a woman will be treated as in the same employment if the man is employed by the woman's employer or any associated employer at the same establishment or establishments in Great Britain which include that one and at which common terms and conditions of employment are observed. The requirement is to show common terms and conditions in respect of the two establishments rather than between the man and the woman. Two employers are associated with each other if one of them controls the other or both are controlled by a third party. The meaning of 'establishment' is assessed with reference to certain factors, namely the degree of permanence, whether there is exclusive occupation of premises and whether there is some organisation of people working there. Therefore, there is no need for both the male and female to be working at the same premises and they may be working across different sites.

REVISION NOTE

The issue of an employee's pay is also conditioned by the common law right of an employee to be paid where they are ready and willing to work. Statutory provisions such as the National Minimum Wage Act 1998 and Part II of the Employment Rights Act 1996 on the unauthorised deduction of wages should also be borne in mind.

■ 'Like work'

Section 1(2)(a) of the EPA 1970 defines one of the components of the equality clause. The equality clause operates when a woman is employed on 'like work' with a man in the same employment. For the purposes of determining whether a man and woman are employed on 'like work', s. 1(4) provides that their work must be the same or broadly similar. Work will be 'broadly similar' if the differences between their work are of no practical importance. Moreover, the nature, extent and frequency of the differences must be taken into account.

KEY CASE

Capper Pass Ltd v. Lawton [1976] IRLR 366

Concerning: 'like work'

Facts

A female employee worked as a cook 40 hours a week unsupervised. She prepared and served lunches for between 10 and 20 persons. An assistant chef supervised by a head chef worked 45 hours per week in the canteen and

---

▶

KEY CASE

prepared 350 meals a day. It was agreed that the female and male were not engaged in like work, but was their work 'broadly similar'?

Legal principle

It was held that the differences in work between the cook and the assistant chef were of no practical importance and that the work was broadly similar. Accordingly, the 'like work' test in s. 1(2)(a) of the EPA 1970 had been satisfied.

■ 'Work rated as equivalent'

Section 1(2)(b) of the EPA 1970 sets out the second component of the equality clause. The equality clause will operate when a woman is employed on work rated as equivalent with a man in the same employment. Here, the jobs of the man and the woman are clearly different. Section 1(5) provides that the work of a woman and a man will be rated as equivalent if their jobs have been given an equal value in terms of demand (based on the criteria of effort, skill and decision-making) as part of a voluntary, impartial and suitably analytical job evaluation scheme. There is no compulsion on an employer to produce such a study.

KEY CASE

Springboard Sunderland Trust v. *Robson* [1992] IRLR 261

Concerning: 'work rated as equivalent'

Facts

A female employee worked as a team leader and sought to compare herself with a male induction officer. She scored 410 points (after her appeal from 400 points was upheld). The male induction officer scored 428 points. Grade 3 was banded as 360–409 points and grade 4 as 410–449 points. The question was whether their jobs were rated as equivalent.

Legal principle

She was entitled to compare herself with the male induction officer. This was on the basis that their work was rated as equivalent. She was allocated within the same grade as the male. Hence, the differences in the scores were not significant.

■ 'Work of equal value'

The third component of the equality clause is outlined in s. 1(2)(c) of the EPA 1970. The equality clause will operate when a woman is employed on work of equal value (based on factors such as effort, skill and decision-making) with a man in the same employment.

The relationship between 'work of equal value' and 'work rated as equivalent'

The 'work of equal value' component was introduced in 1983 by the UK Government. It was introduced to comply with Article 141 of the EC Treaty, since under the pre-1983 law there was no mechanism other than the 'work rated as equivalent' criterion to enable a female employee to compare herself with a male employee doing a different job. Since the job evaluation scheme which forms the basis of the 'work rated as equivalent' test is (and was) purely voluntary, there was no basis on which a female employee could force an employer to grade different jobs in terms of demands such as effort, skill and decision-making. Section 1(2)(c) of the EPA 1970 fills the gap by enabling a female employee who believes that her work is of equal value with that of a man doing a different job to ascertain the validity of her claim. An employment tribunal has the power to select and appoint an independent expert to carry out a job evaluation study.

■ Genuine material factor defence

Once a female employee has:

■ identified a suitable male comparator;
■ demonstrated that one of her terms is less generous than his; and
■ demonstrated that one of the 'like work', 'work rated as equivalent' or 'work of equal value' tests has been satisfied,

a rebuttable presumption of unequal pay or sex discrimination in pay arises. The onus then falls on the employer to rebut that presumption. This is achieved by demonstrating that the pay differential is genuinely due to a material factor which is completely gender neutral.

Genuine material factors?

Case law has established a number of material factors which may be genuine and which are gender neutral. See Figure 7.1.

Figure 7.1

Case name	Legal principle
Cadman [2006] IRLR 969	Rebuttable presumption that length of service is a 'GMF'
Jørgensen [2000] IRLR 726	Budgetary constraints cannot be a 'GMF'
Rainey [1987] IRLR 26	Rebuttable presumption that market forces are 'GMFs'
Enderby [1993] IRLR 591	Where collective agreement results in pay disparities, this is unlikely to be 'GMF'

What if the genuine material factor is not gender neutral?

If the female employee can provide evidence that the material factor is not gender neutral but that it in fact functions in a way which is discriminatory or exhibits a direct or indirect discriminatory impact, then the onus reverts to the employer to objectively justify the difference in the terms of the female and of the male employee. See Figure 7.2. This is the position in the domestic courts under the EPA 1970 (*Glasgow City Council* v. *Marshall* (2000), *Villalba* v. *Merrill Lynch* (2006) and *Armstrong* v. *Newcastle upon Tyne NHS Hospital Trust* (2006).

FURTHER THINKING

However, the domestic position is arguably inconsistent with EC law jurisprudence: see *Brunnhofer* v. *Bank der Österreichischen Postsparkasse AG* [2001] IRLR 571 and *Sharp* v. *Caledonia Group Services Ltd* (2006). EC jurisprudence requires an employer to objectively justify whether a genuine material factor resulting in a pay disparity is gender neutral or not.

Figure 7.2

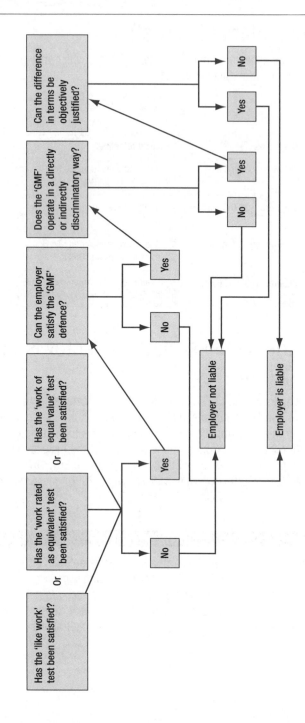

■ Article 141 of the EC Treaty and the Equal Pay Directive

Article 141 of the EC Treaty must also be considered. It imposes an obligation on the UK and other member states to ensure that the principle of equal pay for male and female workers for equal work or work of equal value applies. While Article 141 may be used in domestic courts to interpret domestic law which is inconsistent with EC law, it confers no separate free-standing right. The Equal Pay Directive is directly effective against emanations of the state. Meanwhile, Article 141 is directly effective against public or private employers. If any provision of the EPA 1970 (or indeed the Sex Discrimination Act 1975) is incompatible with EC law the claimant is entitled to rely directly on the EC provisions and case law and to argue that the incompatible domestic provision should be disapplied.

Problem area Article 141: Do the female or male comparators require to work for the same employer? The 'single source'.

There are circumstances when a claim must fail even where the female and male have the same employer. In *Lawrence* v. *Regent Office Care Ltd* (2002), the ECJ held that where differences in pay or conditions cannot be attributed to a single source, there is no body which is responsible for the inequality and which could restore equal treatment. Therefore, such a situation does not come within the compass of Article 141. In *Robertson* v. *DEFRA* (2005), the 'single source' test was applied to deny female civil servants in one Government department from comparing themselves with male civil servants in another Government department – even though they had the same employer, i.e. the Crown. The Court of Appeal came to the same conclusion that a female employee could not compare herself with a male employee – where they both had the same employer in the case of *Armstrong* v. *Newcastle upon Tyne Hospitals NHS Trust* (2006). Here the equal pay claim of a female employee working for an NHS Trust failed under Article 141 on the basis of the absence of a 'single source'. She had attempted to compare herself with a male employee working for the same NHS Trust at a different hospital (although they had originally worked for two different NHS Trusts, which had then merged).

Chapter summary
Putting it all together

☐ Can you tick all the points from the revision checklist at the beginning of this chapter?

☐ Take the **end-of-chapter quiz** on the companion website.

☐ Test your knowledge of the cases below with the **revision flashcards** on the website.

☐ Attempt the essay question at the beginning of the chapter using the guidelines below.

☐ Go to the companion website to try out other questions.

Answer guidelines

See the essay question at the start of this chapter. A diagram illustrating how to structure your answer is available on the website.

Points to remember when answering this question:

■ Clarify that the EPA 1970 is about the pay-related terms of men and women doing 'like work', 'work rated as equivalent' or 'work of equal value' being different.

■ Exploring the key concepts of 'like work', 'work rated as equivalent' or 'work of equal value' is essential.

■ Include a discussion centred around criteria which qualify as 'genuine material factors'.

■ Examine the relationship and differences between the regimes under the EPA 1970 and Article 141 of the EC Treaty, i.e. difference in the stages at which objective justification must take place – see Figure 7.2 above.

Make your answer stand out

■ Address the desirability of a single equality statute in the context of equal pay.

■ Consider whether domestic law conforms with the 'single source' test in EC law and whether UK law is in breach of EC law in failing to compel an employer to objectively justify at an earlier stage in the 'GMF' process – see Figure 7.2.

8
Wrongful dismissal

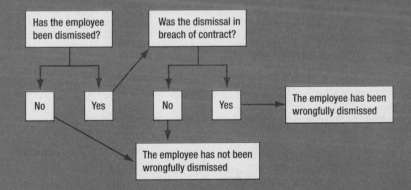

Revision Checklist

What you need to know:

☐ When a dismissal will be wrongful

☐ How wrongful dismissal claims are enforced

☐ The difference between wrongful dismissal and unfair dismissal

☐ What can and cannot be compensated under a wrongful dismissal claim.

Introduction:
Understanding wrongful dismissal

An employee has a common law right not to be wrongfully dismissed.

This chapter examines the concept of wrongful dismissal which exists at common law. It analyses when a dismissed employee will be entitled to raise a wrongful dismissal claim. An employee will be deemed to have been wrongfully dismissed when:

1. the employee has been dismissed; and
2. the dismissal was in repudiatory breach of contract on the part of the employer.

A common example is where an employee is dismissed without notice or with less notice than they are contractually entitled to receive.

Essay question advice

Essays require broad general knowledge of the principles of wrongful dismissal and how such claims are enforced. You will also be expected to know the difference between a wrongful dismissal claim and a claim for unfair dismissal. The key difference is that a wrongful dismissal claim exists at *common law* only and is usually enforced in the courts, whereas an unfair dismissal claim is a *statutory claim* which can only be enforced in an employment tribunal. See Figure 8.1 for the other differences between the two claims. A number of cases have explored the losses which may be compensated under a claim of wrongful dismissal. Essay questions may require you to deal with these issues in some detail.

Problem question advice

A question may involve an examination of the facts with a view to determining whether an individual who has been dismissed has a reasonable prospect of success in pursuing a wrongful dismissal claim, i.e. that an employee has been dismissed (or constructively dismissed) in breach of contract. The problem question may also list a number of losses sustained by the dismissed individual. You may be required to analyse whether the law permits the individual to be compensated in respect of such losses.

Sample question

Could you answer this question? Below is a typical problem question that could arise on this topic. Guidelines on answering the question are included at the end of the chapter, whilst a sample essay question and guidance on tackling it can be found on the companion website.

Problem question

Hugh has worked for Offdesk Plc for ten months as a senior bond trader. His contract of employment states that his employer must give him four months' prior notice of dismissal and he is entitled to be paid a guaranteed bonus so long as he is employed at the bonus payment date – which is only five weeks away. Hugh is Mary's line manager. A serious allegation is made against him by Mary. Hugh's employer's reaction is immediately to suspend him. No investigation into the allegations is undertaken. Six days after the making of the allegation Hugh is summoned to a meeting with the human resources director and chairman of the employer. The human resources director verbally abuses him in front of the chairman and calls him 'completely useless and incompetent from day one'. The chairman explains that the employer believes that the allegations made by Mary are 'a pack of lies'. However, they have nonetheless decided to dismiss Hugh and hand a letter over to him. He is asked to clear his desk and immediately remove himself from the premises. Outside the building, Hugh notes that the letter includes a cheque made payable to him. It explains that the cheque comprises his wages to the date of dismissal (i.e. that very day) and that the reason for his dismissal is incompetence. As a result of the whole experience, Hugh suffers a psychiatric injury. Advise Hugh.

The meaning of 'wrongful dismissal'

KEY DEFINITIONS

Wrongful dismissal: A dismissal of an employee which amounts to a repudiatory breach of contract on the part of the employer.

Unfair dismissal: The dismissal of an employee which is unfair in terms of Part X of the Employment Rights Act 1996 (see Chapter 9 for further details).

An employee is wrongfully dismissed when he is dismissed by his employer in breach of his contract of employment. A wrongful dismissal most commonly occurs where an employee is dismissed without notice or with less notice than the employee is entitled to receive. Another situation where an employee may be held to have been wrongfully dismissed is where they are working on the basis of a fixed-term contract and it is terminated before the expiry date. The key thing to consider is whether:

▌ the employee has been dismissed; and
▌ the dismissal was in repudiatory breach of contract on the part of the employer.

For an example of wrongful dismissal, see *McLelland* v. *Northern Ireland General Health Services Board* (1957).

KEY DEFINITIONS

Fixed-term contract: A contract which endures for a specific period of time and terminates at the end of that period of time.

Repudiatory breach of contract: A breach of a term of a contract which goes to the root of that contract so that on the occurrence of breach the innocent party may be regarded as discharged from further performance of their obligations under the contract.

REVISION NOTE

In Chapter 4, we explored the minimum periods of notice of termination which an employee is entitled to receive from an employer. These minimum periods of notice are based on statute (s. 86(1) of the Employment Rights Act 1996 ('ERA 1996')). If the period of the employee's continuous employment with the employer is less than two years, they are entitled to one week's notice. Thereafter, they are entitled to an extra week's notice for every extra year they have been continuously employed by their employer. This is subject to a maximum limit of 12 weeks' notice. The terms of the employee's written contract of employment may increase the period of notice.

■ The enforcement of wrongful dismissal claims

Claims for wrongful dismissal are essentially common law claims. Hence, they are enforceable in the courts. However, in terms of s. 3 of the ERA 1996, the Employment Tribunals Extension of Jurisdiction (England and Wales) Order 1994 and the Industrial Tribunals Extension of Jurisdiction (Scotland) Order 1994, wrongful dismissal claims may also be enforced in the employment tribunals. However, enforcing a wrongful dismissal claim in an employment tribunal will not always be an attractive route for an employee since compensation is capped at a maximum of £25,000 per claim.

■ The difference between 'wrongful dismissal' claims and unfair dismissal complaints

When an employee has been dismissed, her legal advisers will require to decide whether:

■ to raise a wrongful dismissal claim in the courts or employment tribunal; or
■ to present a complaint to an employment tribunal for unfair dismissal, which Part X of the ERA 1996 states can only be enforced in an employment tribunal.

REVISION NOTE

In Chapter 10, we discuss the statutory disciplinary and dismissal procedures which an employer must comply with prior to dismissing an employee. If an employee enforces their wrongful dismissal claim in the employment tribunal, their award of damages will be increased if the employer has failed to follow these statutory procedures.

EXAM TIP

Should the employee raise a wrongful dismissal claim or complain of unfair dismissal? There are many differences between a common law claim for wrongful dismissal and a statutory claim for unfair dismissal. Where an employee is dismissed, he will have the option of presenting both a wrongful dismissal and an unfair dismissal claim and will be required to choose between them. An employee who has been dismissed must choose whether to raise proceedings based on one or the other. Figure 8.1 outlines the differences between the two and can be used to decide which proceedings to raise.

Figure 8.1

Unfair dismissal	Wrongful dismissal
1. Stautory right	1. Common law right
2. Enforced in employment tribunals	2. Enforced in courts and can only be enforced in tribunal if claim is less than £25,000
3. Maximum limit on compensation (currently £69,900)	3. Unlimited compensation
4. Individual must be an employee	4. Not essential that individual is an employee
5. Individual must have been continuously employed for at least one year	5. No prerequisite of a minimum length of service
6. Individuals employed in certain industry sectors or trades are excluded from the right not to be unfairly dismissed	6. No exclusions from right based on industry sectors or trades
7. Individual can claim unfair dismissal even though he has been dismissed with due notice of termination or a fixed-term contract has expired without renewal	7. It is not possible to claim wrongful dismissal where an employee has been given due notice or a fixed-term contract has expired without renewal

REVISION NOTE

The topic of wrongful dismissal overlaps with unfair dismissal. You should not consider these topics separately but in tandem.

What can and cannot be compensated under a wrongful dismissal claim

Where an employee suffers monetary losses as a result of being wrongfully dismissed, they can claim compensation from their employer in respect of the following:

■ losses suffered where they (i) have been dismissed without the period of notice of termination to which they are legally entitled and (ii) have not received payment in lieu of notice. For example, if an employee is entitled to four weeks' notice of termination and does not receive this, they should receive four weeks' pay in lieu. If they do not, then they will be entitled to four weeks' pay in compensation pursuant to their wrongful dismissal claim;

■ contractual benefits which they would have been entitled to receive during their notice period, e.g. if the period of notice which they are entitled to receive is four weeks, then they are entitled to be compensated for four weeks' worth of contractual benefits, such as pension benefits, bonus payments, sickness insurance payments, etc.;

■ 'stigma' damages, i.e. losses which they have suffered as a result of their inability to obtain alternative employment in the labour market as a result of the stigma associated with the dishonest or fraudulent practices of their former employer; and

■ losses suffered as a result of events leading up to the dismissal which are in breach of contract, e.g. a breach of an implied term or express term of the contract of employment.

The main head of loss which an employee may sustain is the failure of the employer to pay them in lieu of notice. In other words, where an employer dismisses an employee without (i) permitting them to work out their notice period of four weeks and (ii) paying them four weeks' pay in lieu of notice, that employee will have a claim for four weeks' notice pay in respect of the four-week period of notice to which they were entitled. The case of *Addis* v. *Gramophone Co. Ltd* (1909) is a classic example. The House of Lords held in *Addis* that an employee could only claim damages for arrears of notice pay and other financial losses where they had been wrongfully dismissed.

Lost wages and contractual benefits

Together with arrears of notice pay, an employee may seek damages in respect of wages and other contractual benefits (such as pension benefits, bonus payments, sickness insurance payments, etc.) which they are entitled to receive, but which have not been paid or received. The measure of damages will be a sum equivalent to the wages and contractual benefits which would have been earned, between the time of actual termination and the time which the contract might lawfully have been terminated (by due notice).

'Stigma' damages and injury to feelings

The case of *Addis* v. *Gramophone Co. Ltd* (1909) represents a bar to an employee claiming damages in respect of injury to feelings and mental distress which they have suffered as a result of wrongful dismissal. In addition, *Addis* held that an employee could not claim damages in respect of the difficulties which they might have experienced in gaining alternative employment on the labour market. The case of

Malik v. *BCCI SA* (1997) altered the position in respect of the latter issue. Hence, the law now permits employees to claim compensation for 'stigma' damages.

KEY CASE

Malik v. *BCCI SA* [1997] IRLR 462

Concerning: 'stigma' damages, breach of implied term of mutual trust and confidence

Facts

An employee who previously worked for BCCI could not obtain alternative employment in the labour market because of the 'stigma' associated with him having worked previously for BCCI. BCCI had engaged in fraudulent transactions and practices.

Legal principle

Overturning the principle in *Addis* v. *Gramophone Co. Ltd* (1909), it was held that an employee could be compensated in respect of 'stigma' damages. However, the principle in *Addis* that injury to feelings and mental distress which an employee has suffered cannot be compensated still stands as good law.

REVISION NOTE

The issue of 'stigma' damages is relevant to the discussion of the implied term of mutual trust and confidence in Chapters 2 and 3 (see key definition in Chapter 2). An employee may allege that they are entitled to compensation for 'stigma' damages. This is on the basis that the employer breached the implied term of mutual trust and confidence in running a fraudulent, corrupt and dishonest business.

The act of dismissal and events leading up to it

The cases of *Johnson* v. *Unisys Ltd* (2001) and *Eastwood* v. *Magnox Electric plc* (2004) decided that where the act of, or manner of, the dismissal of an employee breaches an implied term (e.g. the implied term of mutual trust and confidence – see Chapters 2 and 3) of the contract of employment, compensation is barred. For example, if an employer shouts or swears at and/or humiliates an employee when the employee is dismissed and the employee suffers a psychiatric injury as a result, the employee will not be entitled to compensation as a result of this breach of the implied term of mutual trust and confidence. The reason the House of Lords gave for this in *Johnson* is that to award compensation in such circumstances would circumvent the intention of Parliament in introducing limited compensation for dismissal under the unfair dismissal regime in Part X of the ERA 1996.

However, where events leading up to the dismissal (e.g. the suspension of the employee, investigations regarding allegations made against the employee or the disciplinary hearing of the employee) are conducted by the employer in a manner which amounts to a breach of an implied term (e.g. the implied term of mutual trust and confidence) of the contract of employment and the employee suffers loss as a result, the employee may be compensated in respect of such losses.

REVISION NOTE

The issue of compensation for events leading up to a dismissal depends upon whether there has been a breach of the contract of employment. For these purposes, the implied term of mutual trust and confidence which was considered in Chapters 2 and 3 is important – since a breach of the implied term by the employer will amount to a breach of contract.

EXAM TIP

In a problem question which asks you to consider whether compensation is available to an employee in relation to their dismissal, students should divide the factual series of events into:

(a) the act of dismissal itself; and

(b) events leading up to the dismissal (e.g. the act of suspension, the disciplinary investigation, the disciplinary hearing, the disciplinary appeal hearing, etc.)

If (a) has been conducted in breach of contract, no compensation is available to an employee. However, if any of (b) are undertaken in breach of contract, damages may be claimed by an employee.

Recovery of compensation for loss of opportunity to claim unfair dismissal

In order to qualify for the unfair dismissal right under s. 94(1) of the ERA 1996, an employee must have been continuously employed with their employer for at least one year. If the employer deliberately dismisses the employee prior to the one-year threshold, can an employee claim compensation from the employer in respect of the loss of opportunity to bring a claim for unfair dismissal under the bracket of a wrongful dismissal claim? See *Virgin Net*.

Virgin Net Ltd v. *Harper* [2004] IRLR 390

Concerning: loss of opportunity to claim unfair dismissal

Facts

Miss Harper's contract of employment provided that she was entitled to three months' notice of termination. She was dismissed without receiving notice of termination 33 days short of the date when she would have completed the one-year period of employment qualifying her to bring a claim of unfair dismissal. She raised a wrongful dismissal claim and sought compensation for the loss of the opportunity to claim unfair dismissal.

Legal principle

The Court of Appeal held that Miss Harper was not entitled to be compensated in respect of the loss of opportunity to claim unfair dismissal. In fact, the Court of Appeal went so far as to say that she had not lost the right to claim compensation for unfair dismissal by being dismissed without her contractual notice. She never had such a right in the first place because she fell short of the requirement of one year's continuous service which Parliament had prescribed.

Recovery of compensation for contractually guaranteed payments

Where an employee's contract of employment provides that they are entitled to a 'guaranteed' bonus payment (or some other form of remuneration) and they are dismissed by their employer as a means of avoiding the payment of such bonus, this will amount to a breach of contract. As a result, the employee may recover compensation. An 'anti-avoidance' implied term of the contract of employment appears to be emerging. In other words, an employer is under an implied duty not to terminate the employment of an employee in order to avoid the operation of an express term which sanctions the making of certain or conditional payments to the employee. See *Jenvey* v. *Australian Broadcasting Corporation* (2002).

The rule in *Johnson* v. *Unisys Ltd* (2001) and *Eastwood* v. *Magnox Electric plc* (2004) that an employee cannot recover compensation in respect of the act of, or the manner of, the dismissal has caused a lot controversy. The principal reason which Lords Nicholls, Hoffmann and Millett in the House of Lords in *Johnson* and *Eastwood* invoked for deciding not to extend the law is that it would ultimately operate in a way to circumvent the statutory unfair dismissal regime in Part X of the ERA 1996 – which imposes a maximum statutory limit on compensation. Do you agree with this?

■ L. Barmes (2004) 'The Continuing Conceptual Crisis in the Common Law of the Contract of Employment', *Modern Law Review* 435
■ H. Collins (2001) 'Claim for Unfair Dismissal', 30 *Industrial Law Journal* 305.

Chapter summary
Putting it all together

☐ Can you tick all the points from the revision checklist at the beginning of this chapter?

☐ Take the **end-of-chapter quiz** on the companion website.

☐ Test your knowledge of the cases below with the **revision flashcards** on the website.

☐ Attempt the essay question at the beginning of the chapter using the guidelines below.

☐ Go to the companion website to try out other questions.

Answer guidelines

See the problem question at the start of this chapter. A diagram illustrating how to structure your answer is available on the website.

■ Your introduction should provide that the employee has a claim for wrongful dismissal and you should then go on to consider the losses in respect of which compensation may be sought.
■ First, the employee will have a claim for four months' pay – he was dismissed without working out his four months' notice period and was not offered four

months' payment in lieu of notice which amounts to a breach of the contract of employment.

■ The employee was dismissed before the one-year qualifying period for unfair dismissal. Consider whether he can claim compensation in respect of the loss of the opportunity to claim unfair dismissal.

■ Analyse whether the employee can claim compensation in respect of psychiatric injury caused by (i) the events leading up to the dismissal and/or (ii) the manner of the dismissal.

■ Consider the position in respect of the employee's lost bonus entitlement.

Make your answer stand out

■ Consider the implications of *Johnson* v. *Unisys Ltd* (2001) and *Eastwood* v. *Magnox Electric plc* (2004). Is it satisfactory that the employee may claim damages for psychiatric injury caused by the events leading up to the dismissal, but not for the actual dismissal itself or the manner of that dismissal?

9
Unfair dismissal (1): basic concepts

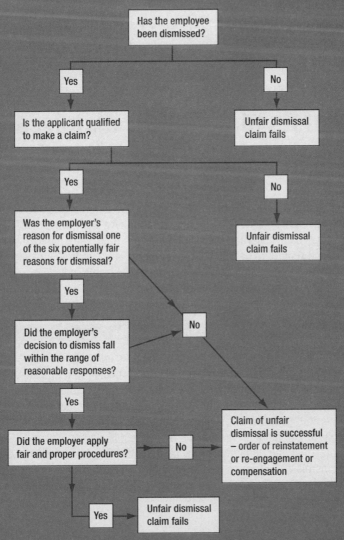

Has the employee been dismissed?

Yes → Is the applicant qualified to make a claim?

No → Unfair dismissal claim fails

Yes → Was the employer's reason for dismissal one of the six potentially fair reasons for dismissal?

No → Unfair dismissal claim fails

Yes → Did the employer's decision to dismiss fall within the range of reasonable responses?

No →

No → Claim of unfair dismissal is successful – order of reinstatement or re-engagement or compensation

Yes → Did the employer apply fair and proper procedures?

No → Claim of unfair dismissal is successful – order of reinstatement or re-engagement or compensation

Yes → Unfair dismissal claim fails

Revision Checklist

What you need to know:

- [ ] The qualifying criteria for an unfair dismissal claim
- [ ] The automatically unfair dismissals
- [ ] The method of enforcement of unfair dismissal claims
- [ ] The three definitions of dismissal in s. 95(1) of the Employment Rights Act 1996
- [ ] The six valid reasons for dismissal in s. 98(1) and (2) of the Employment Rights Act 1996
- [ ] How the 'range of reasonable responses' test operates in practice
- [ ] The importance of fair and proper disciplinary procedures and policies.

Introduction:
Understanding unfair dismissal

An employee has a statutory right not to be unfairly dismissed.

This chapter examines the right of an employee not to be unfairly dismissed. It analyses the circumstances when a dismissed employee will have a reasonable prospect of success in asserting their statutory right not to be unfairly dismissed. The processes which require to be followed in terms of Part X of the Employment Rights Act 1996 in order to determine whether a dismissal is prima facie fair or unfair will be examined. Finally, we will consider the proper and fair disciplinary procedures and policies which an employer must follow prior to the dismissal of an employee.

Essay question advice

Essays require broad general knowledge of the principles of unfair dismissal and how such claims are enforced. You may also be expected to know the qualifying criteria for a claim for unfair dismissal and have an understanding of the automatically unfair dismissals. The statutory definition of 'dismissal' must also be understood, together with the six statutory reasons for dismissal. An appreciation of the 'range of reasonable responses' is also crucial and demonstrates that you understand how courts and tribunals come to a view whether a dismissal is prima facie fair or unfair. The importance of fair and proper disciplinary procedures must also be understood and explored.

Problem question advice

Problem questions may involve the examination of a particular individual employee's or employer's factual situation with a view to determining whether an individual who has been dismissed has a reasonable prospect of success in pursuing an unfair dismissal claim in an employment tribunal. In answering the problem question, you will require to keep in mind (i) the qualifying criteria for an unfair dismissal claim and (ii) automatically unfair dismissals. You should also be able to assess whether the facts amount to a 'dismissal' and whether the reason for dismissal is one of the six statutory reasons for dismissal. In coming to a view as to whether a dismissal is prima facie fair or unfair, problem questions may require you (i) to explain and apply the 'range of reasonable responses' test and (ii) to assess whether the procedures applied by the employer were fair and proper.

Sample question

Could you answer this question? Below is a typical essay question that could arise on this topic. Guidelines on answering the question are included at the end of the chapter, whilst a sample problem question and guidance on tackling it can be found on the companion website.

Essay question

Evaluate how the 'range of reasonable responses' test applies in practice. Explain whether you believe this test is a 'perversity' test.

KEY DEFINITION

Unfair dismissal The dismissal of an employee which is unfair in terms of Part X of the Employment Rights Act 1996 ('ERA 1996').

■ The qualifying criteria for unfair dismissal

In order to be eligible to present a complaint of unfair dismissal to an employment tribunal, an individual must:

■ be an employee;
■ have been continuously employed for one year or more (s. 108 of the ERA 1996);
■ not be employed in the police service or the armed forces; and
■ be employed in Great Britain.

EXAM TIP

In a problem question which concerns an employee who has been dismissed, you must ensure that each of the above four qualifying criteria have been satisfied. Otherwise, the dismissed employee will not be entitled to bring a claim for unfair dismissal. If you are not told so, you should not assume that the employee's length of service is more or less than one year.

■ Enforcement of unfair dismissal claims

Section 111(1) of the ERA 1996 provides that unfair dismissal claims are to be enforced in the employment tribunals.

KEY STATUTORY PROVISION

ERA 1996, s. 111(1)

A complaint may be presented to an employment tribunal against an employer by any person that he was unfairly dismissed by the employer.

Hence, an employee is not entitled to raise an action of unfair dismissal in the courts. The reason is that Parliament intended for unfair dismissal claims to be dealt with by specialist employment tribunals which are experienced in the resolution of such disputes.

■ Automatically unfair dismissals

Where any of the following criteria are met (this list is not exhaustive), a dismissal will be automatically unfair and the period of one year's continuous employment of the employee is irrelevant in such circumstances:

■ The employer failed to implement the statutory minimum standard dismissal and disciplinary procedure or the statutory minimum modified dismissal and disciplinary procedure contained in chapters 1 and 2 of Part 1 of Sch. 2 to the Employment Act 2002 – s. 98A(1) of the ERA 1996.

■ The employee is dismissed on the basis that he was a member of a **trade union** or was not a member of a trade union – s. 152 of the Trade Union and Labour Relations (Consolidation) Act 1992.

■ The employee is dismissed for a reason connected with pregnancy, childbirth or maternity – s. 99 of the ERA 1996.

■ The employee is dismissed for a reason connected with health and safety, e.g.

where an employee makes a complaint to his employer about a breach of health and safety laws – s. 100 of the ERA 1996.
- The employee is dismissed for taking action to exercise one of his rights under the Working Time Regulations 1998, e.g. a breach of the 48-hour working week – s. 101A of the Employment Rights Act 1996.
- The employee is dismissed for asserting one of his statutory rights, e.g. an employee's statutory right to time off work to look after dependants under s. 57A of the ERA 1996 – s. 104 of the ERA 1996.

The meaning of 'dismissal'

There are three types of 'dismissal'. If an employee cannot show that he has been 'dismissed', his claim for unfair dismissal will be ruled out by an employment tribunal.

KEY STATUTORY PROVISION

ERA 1996, s. 95(1)

... an employee is dismissed by his employer if –

(a) the contract under which he is employed is terminated by the employer (whether with or without notice),

(b) he is employed under a limited-term contract and that contract terminates by virtue of the limiting event without being renewed under the same contract, or

(c) the employee terminates the contract under which he is employed (with or without notice) in circumstances in which he is entitled to terminate it without notice by reason of the employer's conduct.

REVISION NOTE

Section 95(1)(a) of the ERA 1996 entails a positive act of dismissal by the employer, i.e. where the employer 'fires' the employee. Section 95(1)(b) applies where a fixed-term contract comes to its natural end. Finally, s. 95(1)(c) describes the constructive dismissal of an employee – a concept to be explored in greater detail in Chapter 10.

KEY DEFINITION

Fixed-term contract A contract which endures for a specific period of time and terminates at the end of that period of time.

The six potentially fair reasons for dismissal

Section 98(1), (2) and (3) provide six potentially fair reasons for dismissal. An employer must show that the reason they dismissed an employee was for one of the following six reasons:

I some other substantial reason;
I the capability or qualifications of the employee;
I the conduct of the employee;
I the retirement of the employee;
I the redundancy of the employee; or
I the contravention of a duty or statute.

If the employer is unable to show that the reason for the dismissal is one of the above, the dismissal will be held to be unfair.

'Some other substantial reason'

What factual circumstances amount to 'some other substantial reason' in terms of s. 98(1)(b) of the ERA 1996? First, the reason must not be whimsical. Second, most cases involve the employer dismissing an employee in order to protect their legitimate business interests. Circumstances where the reason for a dismissal of an employee has been held by the tribunals to constitute 'some other substantial reason' have been as follows:

I where an employee was found to have a difficult personality or unfortunate manner (*Perkin* v. *St George's Healthcare NHS Trust* (2005);
I where the employer dismissed the employee at the behest of their key client (*Scott Packing and Warehousing Co Ltd* v. *Paterson* (1978); and
I where the employer dismissed the employee subsequent to a corporate takeover (*Cobley* v. *Forward Technology Industries plc* (2003).

'Capability or qualifications'

The second potentially fair reason for dismissal is 'capability or qualifications'. This involves the illness, poor performance, incompetence or lack of qualifications of an employee. See Figure 9.1 for clarification of the relevant issues to take into account in respect of incompetence and ill-health.

'Conduct'/misconduct

The third potentially fair reason is the 'conduct' of the employee, i.e. gross or serious misconduct (e.g. fighting, intoxication theft, etc., in the workplace), breaches of discipline or procedure or the commission of criminal offences. See Figure 9.2 for clarification of the relevant issues in respect of misconduct.

Retirement

Retirement is the fourth potentially fair reason – and this is subject to the particular regime in ss. 98ZA–98ZH of the ERA 1996 and the Employment Equality (Age) Regulations 2006. See Chapter 6.

Figure 9.1

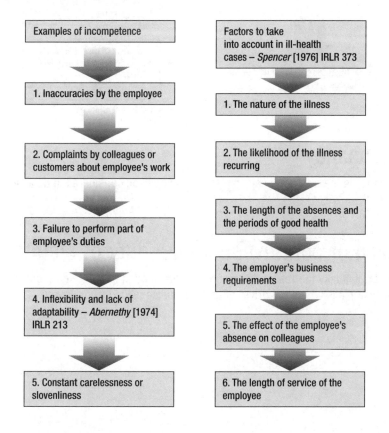

Figure 9.2

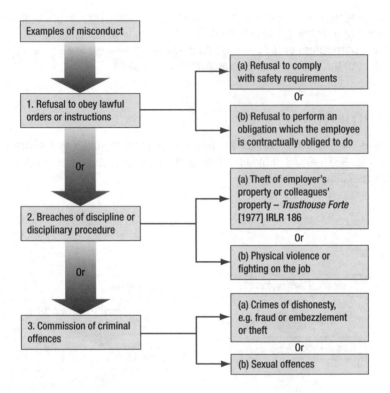

Redundancy

Redundancy is the fifth potentially fair reason and will be considered in detail in Chapter 10.

Breach or contravention of a duty or statute

The final potentially fair reason is breach or contravention of a duty or statute. A simple example is where the driver of an HGV is disqualified from driving.

■ The 'range of reasonable responses' test

Once the employer has shown that the reason for the dismissal of the employee was one of the above six reasons, they must satisfy the employment tribunal that their decision to dismiss fell within the band of reasonable responses open to them.

KEY STATUTORY PROVISION

ERA 1996, s. 98(4)

(4) In any other case where the employer has fulfilled the requirements of subsection (1), the determination of the question whether the dismissal is fair or unfair (having regard to the reason shown by the employer) –

(a) depends on whether in the circumstances (including the size and administrative resources of the employer's undertaking) the employer acted reasonably or unreasonably in treating it as a sufficient reason for dismissing the employee, and

(b) shall be determined in accordance with equity and the substantial merits of the case.

The reasonableness or unreasonableness of the employer

In construing whether a dismissal is fair or unfair, the tribunals apply the 'range of reasonable responses' test. Instead of the tribunal or court enquiring whether the employer's decision to dismiss was reasonable or unreasonable on a purely objective basis and thus substituting their own judgment for that of the employer, the tribunal must ask whether dismissal was one of the reasonable responses which an employer might take to the act complained of, the events which occurred or the reason for the employee's dismissal. For an example of the range of reasonable responses test in operation, see Figure 9.3.

Figure 9.3

Case study No. 1
Scenario: Employee is dismissed for misconduct for claiming travel expenses of £600 when employer's investigation reveals no suggestion of fraud. She submits only £580 of receipts.
Question: What are the reasonable responses of an employer to this event/reason?
Employment tribunal identifies three reasonable responses: 1. Employer takes no action. 2. Employer issues a verbal warning. 3. Employer obtains employee's agreement to the deduction of £20 from her wages.
Outcome: Since dismissal is not identified as a reasonable response, dismissal is prima facie unfair.

Case study No. 2
Scenario: Employee is dismissed on capability grounds. Employee is a doctor and performed surgery on a patient's wrong kidney.
Question: What are the reasonable responses of an employer to this event/reason?
Employment Tribunal identifies two reasonable responses: 1. Dismissal 2. Final written warning
Outcome: Since dismissal is identified as a reasonable response, dismissal is prima facie fair.

KEY CASE

British Home Stores Ltd v. *Burchell* [1978] IRLR 379

Concerning: 'range of reasonable responses' test, misconduct of employee

Facts

Burchell was dismissed for allegedly being involved with a number of other employees in acts of dishonesty relating to staff purchases. The employer conducted an investigation into allegations of irregularities and, during the investigation, Burchell was implicated by another of the employees involved.

▶

Legal principle

The EAT held that Burchell's dismissal was not unfair. The 'range of reasonable responses' test was applied by the EAT. Guidance on the approach which tribunals should take in cases of misconduct was elaborated upon as follows:

1. the employer must demonstrate that they believed that the employee was guilty of the relevant misconduct at the time they took the decision to dismiss;
2. the employer must demonstrate that they had in mind reasonable grounds upon which to sustain that belief; and
3. the employer, at the stage at which they formed that belief on those grounds, and at any rate at the final stage at which they formed that belief on those grounds, must have carried out as much investigation into the matter as was reasonable in all the circumstances of the case.

EXAM TIP

A problem question may ask you to consider a set of facts and circumstances relating to an individual employee who has been dismissed. In answering the problem question and analysing whether the dismissal is fair or unfair, you should concentrate on the reason for the dismissal and ask what the responses of a reasonable employer to that reason or act would have been. As shown in Figure 9.3, you should then jot down what those reasonable responses might be. If dismissal does not feature within the range, then the dismissal is unfair.

FURTHER THINKING

Judicial and academic commentators have criticised the 'range of reasonable responses' test and the hurdles which it places in front of dismissed employees. Do you agree with Collins that 'in practice, it often degenerates into a test of perversity... [and] upholds the justice of dismissals that are "harsh but fair"'?

- H. Collins (2000) 'Finding the Right Direction for the Industrial Jury', 29 *Industrial Law Journal* 288
- H. Collins (2004) *Nine Proposals for the Reform of the Law on Unfair Dismissal*. London: Institute of Employment Rights.

Fair and proper dismissal and disciplinary procedures and policies

Where an employer fails to comply with either of the statutory disciplinary procedures in Part 1 of Sch. 2 to the Employment Act 2002 prior to the dismissal of an employee, s. 98A(1) of the ERA 1996 provides that this will amount to an automatically unfair dismissal. In other words, the employee will not require to show that there has been a dismissal and that the dismissal was fair.

The content of the statutory procedures

The procedures contained in the statutory standard dismissal and disciplinary procedure and the statutory modified dismissal and disciplinary procedure are fairly basic. For example, the statutory standard dismissal and disciplinary procedure consists of a basic three-stage process:

1. written warning of the contemplation of dismissal;
2. disciplinary hearing; and
3. appeal hearing.

Problem area Which statutory procedure?

Whether an employer requires to follow the statutory standard dismissal and disciplinary procedure in chapter 1 of Part 1 of Sch. 2 to the Employment Act 2002 or the statutory modified dismissal and disciplinary procedure contained in chapter 2 of Part 1 of Sch. 2 to the Employment Act 2002 is determined by reg. 3 of the Employment Act 2002 (Dispute Resolution) Regulations 2004. This provides that the statutory modified procedure is only to be used where the employer has already dismissed the employee without notice or any payment in lieu of notice. Meanwhile, the statutory procedure applies where the employer is contemplating dismissal.

Non-statutory fair and proper procedures and policies

A distinction must be made between (i) the statutory dismissal procedures and (ii) the non-statutory dismissal procedures and policies. Even if the employer complies with (i), they must apply (ii), otherwise the dismissal of an employee is likely be held to be

Figure 9.4

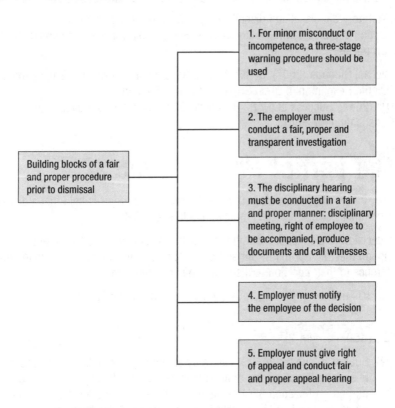

Building blocks of a fair and proper procedure prior to dismissal

1. For minor misconduct or incompetence, a three-stage warning procedure should be used

2. The employer must conduct a fair, proper and transparent investigation

3. The disciplinary hearing must be conducted in a fair and proper manner: disciplinary meeting, right of employee to be accompanied, produce documents and call witnesses

4. Employer must notify the employee of the decision

5. Employer must give right of appeal and conduct fair and proper appeal hearing

unfair by an employment tribunal. The non-statutory dismissal procedures are more elaborate fair and proper procedures than the statutory dismissal procedures and are often contained in an employer's contractual disciplinary procedure – which may be based on the ACAS Code of Practice. Tribunals are extremely clear that the application of good industrial practice – and the compliance of employers with fair and reasonable non-statutory dismissal procedures – is crucial to a finding of fair dismissal. The upshot of this is that if the employer's decision to dismiss is found to fall within the band of reasonable responses, the dismissal will nevertheless be deemed to be unfair if the employer failed to follow fair and proper non-statutory dismissal procedures. See Figure 9.4 for the basic building blocks of such a fair and proper procedure.

The statutory dismissal and disciplinary procedures have been criticised as too formal and complex by practising lawyers. See the following recommendations and proposals:

- Michael Gibbons (2007) 'Better Dispute Resolution: A Review of Employment Dispute Resolution in Great Britain' (March, DTI); and
- DTI (2007) 'Success at Work: Resolving Disputes in the Workplace – A Consultation' (March).

■ The partial *Polkey* reversal

In *Polkey* v. *A.E. Dayton Services Ltd* (1987), the House of Lords held that a dismissal would be unfair, even where an employer could show that:

- the decision to dismiss fell within the range of reasonable responses; and
- although they did not follow fair and proper procedures, it would have made no difference to their decision to dismiss if they had done so.

This rule has now been partially reversed by s. 98A(2) of the ERA 1996.

KEY STATUTORY PROVISION
ERA 1996, s. 98A(2) (2) Subject to subsection (1), failure by an employer to follow a procedure in relation to the dismissal of an employee shall not be regarded for the purposes of section 98(4)(a) as by itself making the employer's action unreasonable if he shows that he would have decided to dismiss the employee if he had followed the procedure.

The effect of the partial *Polkey* reversal

The effect of s. 98A(2) can be summarised as follows:

- if the employer complies with the minimum requirements in the statutory standard dismissal and disciplinary procedure in chapter 1 of Part 1 of Sch. 2 to the Employment Act 2002; or
- if the employer complies with the minimum requirements in the statutory modified dismissal and disciplinary procedure in chapter 2 of Part 1 of Sch. 2 to the Employment Act 2002;
- but the employer does not comply with the extra further fair and proper dismissal

and disciplinary procedures contained in either (i) the employer's own contractual or customary disciplinary procedures or (ii) the ACAS Code of Practice;
■ then, provided that they can demonstrate (i) that the decision to dismiss and/or the investigation which they undertook in respect of the misconduct dismissal fell within the 'range of reasonable responses' and (ii) that their failure to follow the fair and proper procedures in 3. above would have made no difference to the outcome,
■ then – the dismissal will nevertheless be held to be fair.

Chapter summary
Putting it all together

TEST YOURSELF

☐ Can you tick all the points from the revision checklist at the beginning of this chapter?

☐ Take the **end-of-chapter quiz** on the companion website.

☐ Test your knowledge of the cases below with the **revision flashcards** on the website.

☐ Attempt the essay question at the beginning of the chapter using the guidelines below.

☐ Go to the companion website to try out other questions.

Answer guidelines

See the essay question at the start of this chapter. A diagram illustrating how to structure your answer is available on the website.

Points to remember when answering this question:

■ In your introduction, you should explore the preliminary stages of an unfair dismissal claim, i.e. (i) whether there has been a 'dismissal' in terms of s. 95(1) of the ERA 1996 and (ii) whether the employer's reason for the dismissal was one of the potentially fair reasons.
■ The method of enforcement of unfair dismissal claims.
■ You should display an understanding of the automatically unfair dismissals.
■ Consider the importance of the application of fair and proper disciplinary procedures.

Make your answer stand out

■ Address whether you believe that the range of reasonable responses test is a perversity test.

■ Examine other tests which could, or perhaps ought to, replace the range of reasonable responses test, e.g. a proportionality test – and what would this mean?

10

Unfair dismissal (2): remedies, constructive dismissal and redundancy

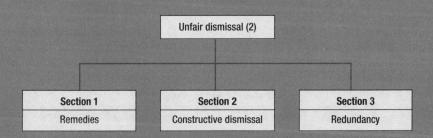

Revision Checklist

What you need to know:

☐ The remedies available to an employee who has been unfairly dismissed

☐ A basic understanding of compensation which can be awarded to an employee who has been unfairly dismissed

☐ How the tribunals and courts determine whether an employee has been constructively dismissed

☐ How the tribunals and courts determine whether an employee has been made redundant.

Introduction:
Understanding remedies, constructive dismissal and redundancy

An employee has a statutory right not to be unfairly constructively dismissed or unfairly dismissed on the basis of redundancy.

This chapter examines the remedies of an employee where an employment tribunal makes a finding that she has been unfairly dismissed. It analyses the main remedy, which is the remedy of compensation. In addition, the circumstances in which an employee has been found to have been constructively dismissed will be examined, together with the processes which the tribunal and court apply in coming to such a decision. It is important that you understand that constructive dismissal is a form of unfair dismissal and so this should be read closely in conjunction with Chapter 9. Finally, the important topic of redundancy will be considered.

Essay question advice

Essays require broad general knowledge of the remedies available to employees and the principles of constructive dismissal. You will also be expected to know the issues which arise where a tribunal or court requires to ascertain whether an employee's claim for constructive dismissal ought to be upheld. You must also appreciate the statutory definition of 'redundancy', since it constitutes one of the six statutory potentially fair reasons for dismissal. An appreciation of the issues which the tribunals will take into account in determining whether an individual has been made redundant and whether the redundancy was fair is also essential.

Problem question advice

Problem questions may involve an examination of a particular individual employee's or employer's factual circumstances with a view to determining whether that individual has a reasonable prospect of success in pursuing (i) a constructive dismissal claim in the employment tribunals or (ii) an unfair dismissal claim on the basis that he or she has not been made redundant. In answering a problem question, you should also be able to assess whether the facts amount to a 'constructive dismissal' or an unfair redundancy and whether the individual who has been dismissed satisfies the definition of 'redundancy' in s. 139 of the Employment Rights Act 1996.

Sample question

Could you answer this question? Below is a typical problem question that could arise on this topic. Guidelines on answering the question are included at the end of the chapter, whilst a sample essay question and guidance on tackling it can be found on the companion website.

Problem question

Glenn Bristow has been employed by FictitiousCorp Ltd as a human resources assistant for six years. He is appraised by his employer every three months and his past nine appraisals have pointed to less than satisfactory performance. Glenn has been issued with appropriate performance criteria after each appraisal. Issues such as his time-keeping, attention to detail and interpersonal skills have consistently been graded poorly and remain a concern. FictitiousCorp Ltd announces that it is to make 15 people redundant (out of a workforce of 500 employees) in their human resources department due to a slowdown in sales and Glenn is earmarked for redundancy. The selection criterion applied by FictitiousCorp Ltd is past performance. Hence, this is the reason why Glenn is selected as one of the unlucky 15. Glenn is not offered suitable alternative employment by FictitiousCorp Ltd. He is not consulted about the proposed redundancy. When he is made redundant and receives a redundancy payment based on the statutory criteria, he seeks your advice regarding his position. Advise Glenn.

∎ Remedies for unfair dismissal

There are three remedies available where an employee has been held to have been unfairly dismissed, namely reinstatement, re-engagement (see s. 113 of the Employment Rights Act 1996 ('ERA 1996')) or compensation. Reinstatement involves the reversal of the dismissal so that the employee gets their old job back.

Re-engagement is slightly different and describes the situation where an employee is re-employed by their employer but works in a different job.

Compensation

In approximately 95% of cases in which an employee is successful in their unfair dismissal claim, compensation will be the remedy awarded by the employment tribunal. Compensation involves the employee being awarded a basic award and compensatory award. The basic award is a fixed figure which can be calculated depending on the employee's length of continuous service and age. At present, the maximum amount payable is £9,300, but such maximum limit is increased annually. The maximum compensatory award is currently fixed at £60,600. Like the basic award, this maximum figure is increased every year. The amount of the compensatory award is defined by s. 123 of the ERA 1996. Section 124A of the ERA 1996 provides that the compensatory award must be increased by at least 10% (and may be increased up to 50%) where the employer has failed to comply with:

▌ the statutory standard dismissal and disciplinary procedure in chapter 1 of Part 1 of Sch. 2 to the Employment Act 2002; or
▌ the statutory modified dismissal and disciplinary procedure contained in chapter 2 of Part 1 of Sch. 2 to the Employment Act 2002.

KEY STATUTORY PROVISION

ERA 1996, s. 123

(1) ... the amount of the compensatory award shall be such amount as the tribunal considers just and equitable in all the circumstances having regard to the loss sustained by the complainant in consequence of the dismissal in so far as that loss is attributable to action taken by the employer.

(2) The loss referred to in subsection (1) shall be taken to include –

   (a) any expenses reasonably incurred by the complainant in consequence of the dismissal, and

   (b) subject to subsection (3), loss of any benefit which he might reasonably be expected to have had but for the dismissal ...

The tribunals and courts have consistently pronounced that the purpose of the compensatory award is to compensate the employee for their financial loss. Its objective is not to penalise the employer for any fault on their part in dismissing the employee.

Problem area Loss?

In *Dunnachie* v. *Kingston-Upon-Hull City Council* (2004), the House of Lords held that it was not competent to award compensation for losses suffered by the employer in respect of injury to feelings. The word 'loss' in s. 123 of the Employment Rights Act 1996 was restricted to economic losses of the employee. Do you agree with this? In the breach of contract case of *Farley* v. *Skinner* (2001), the House of Lords held that damages for non-monetary losses may be awarded to the innocent party in a breach of contract. You should consider *Farley* and whether the ratio in that case can be used as a basis to critique the reasoning of the House of Lords in *Dunnachie* or not.

Constructive dismissals

Constructive dismissal is a form of unfair dismissal. As a result, it is governed by Part X of the ERA 1996. The definition of 'constructive dismissal' is detailed in s. 95 of the ERA 1996.

KEY STATUTORY PROVISION

ERA 1996, s. 95

(1) For the purposes of this Part an employee is dismissed by his employer if . . .

    (c) the employee terminates the contract under which he is employed (with or without notice) in circumstances in which he is entitled to terminate it without notice by reason of the employer's conduct.

The nature of the employer's conduct

Section 95(1)(c) of the ERA 1996 enables an employee to terminate the contract of employment without notice in response to the employer's conduct. The question is what standard of conduct of the employer is relevant for the purposes of the section. The case of *Western Excavating (ECC) Ltd* v. *Sharp* (1978) held that whether the employer's conduct was reasonable or unreasonable was not the appropriate test. Instead, the question was whether the employer's conduct:

▪ amounted to a significant or repudiatory breach of contract going to the root of the contract of employment, or
▪ demonstrated that the employer no longer intended to be bound by one or more of the essential terms of the contract.

Examples of repudiatory conduct

Some examples of repudiatory conduct are as follows:

■ reducing an employee's benefits to a material extent (*Gillies* v. *Richard Daniels & Co.* (1979);
■ reducing an employee's status or salary (*Coleman* v. *S. & W. Baldwin* (1977) and *Industrial Rubber Products* v. *Gillon* (1977));
■ any breach of the implied terms of the contract of employment, e.g. the implied term of mutual trust and confidence, the implied term to exercise reasonable care, etc.

In such circumstances, the employee is entitled to treat himself as:

■ discharged from any further performance, and
■ constructively dismissed, and can seek compensation.

KEY CASE

***Stanley Cole (Wainfleet) Ltd* v. *Sheridan* [2003] IRLR 52**

Concerning: repudiatory conduct, constructive dismissal

Facts

Mrs Sheridan had an altercation with another employee which upset her and made her feel ill. She left the office without permission and was absent for about an hour and a half, including her lunch hour. When she returned, she was told to go home. An investigation and disciplinary hearing took place which resulted in her being issued with a final written warning for leaving the workplace without permission. She claimed constructive dismissal.

Legal principle

The EAT held that the employer had committed a repudiatory breach of contract in giving the employee an unjust and unmerited warning or other disciplinary sanction which was disproportionate to the misconduct of the employee. A final written warning is a severe penalty which is given for conduct which just stops short of that justifying dismissal. However, the employee's misconduct was minor and so the final written warning was disproportionate.

Land Securities Trillium Ltd **v.** *Thornley* **[2005] IRLR 765**

Concerning: repudiatory conduct, constructive dismissal

Facts

Ms Thornley was employed as an in-house architect. Although she had certain management responsibilities, her main duties were those of a 'hands-on' architect. As part of a restructuring, Ms Thornley's duties were altered to a mainly managerial role on the basis of a 'flexibility' clause in her contract of employment. She contended that the alterations were such that she was being asked to perform a different job without her consent. She claimed constructive dismissal.

Legal principle

The employer was in fundamental breach of her contract of employment in imposing a new job description. The job description changed her duties from a hands-on role to a mainly managerial one and had the effect of deskilling her as an architect. Accordingly, she had been constructively dismissed.

Stages involved in constructive dismissal

See Figure 10.1 for a description of the relevant issues which are taken into account where an employee makes a complaint of constructive dismissal. From Figure 10.1, you will note that it is crucial that the employee has complied with the statutory grievance procedure contained in Part 2 of Sch. 2 to the Employment Act 2002. Otherwise, the employee will not be entitled to present a complaint of constructive dismissal. The statutory standard grievance procedure consists of a basic three-stage process:

■ the employee must set out the basis of his grievance in writing and send it or a copy of it to the employer;
■ the employer must invite the employee to a grievance hearing; and
■ if the employee wishes to appeal, he must inform the employer and, in turn, the employer must invite him to attend an appeal hearing.

The tribunals have interpreted the statutory grievance procedures liberally (see *Shergold* v. *Fieldway Medical Centre* (2006), *Galaxy Showers Ltd* v. *Wilson* (2006) and *Canary Wharf Management* v. *Edebi* (2006)).

Figure 10.1

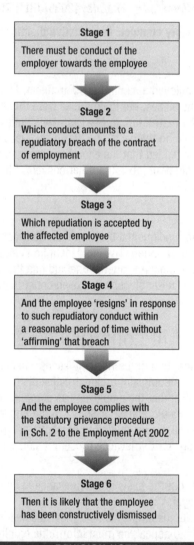

Stage 1

There must be conduct of the employer towards the employee

Stage 2

Which conduct amounts to a repudiatory breach of the contract of employment

Stage 3

Which repudiation is accepted by the affected employee

Stage 4

And the employee 'resigns' in response to such repudiatory conduct within a reasonable period of time without 'affirming' that breach

Stage 5

And the employee complies with the statutory grievance procedure in Sch. 2 to the Employment Act 2002

Stage 6

Then it is likely that the employee has been constructively dismissed

REVISION NOTE

Whether the employer's conduct is such that the employee is entitled to claim constructive dismissal depends on whether there has been a repudiatory breach of contract on the part of the employer. This, in turn, directs an enquiry as to whether (i) the conduct of the employer is consistent with a repudiatory breach on their part or (ii) an express or implied term of the contract of employment has been breached. As a result, the implied terms of the employer which were considered in Chapter 2 assume importance here.

REVISION NOTE

It is important that you appreciate that a constructive dismissal is also by definition a wrongful dismissal. So if an employee can show that the conduct of an employer amounts to a repudiatory breach of contract, they must decide whether to raise a wrongful dismissal claim or a constructive dismissal claim. The option they choose will commonly depend on their length of service and the level of compensation they are seeking. See Figure 8.1 for the differences between a wrongful dismissal claim and an unfair dismissal claim (of which constructive dismissal is a form).

Affirmation

If an employee approves of the employer's conduct (which amounts to a repudiatory breach) then they will be deemed to have waived their right to claim constructive dismissal. Such approval is called 'affirmation'. Whether the employee has affirmed or consented to the employer's repudiatory breach is a matter of fact and degree. For example, in the case of *Simms* v. *Sainsburys Supermarkets* (2005), the EAT held that a delay of ten weeks between the date of the employer's repudiatory breach and the date the employee left employment was too long. Hence, there had been affirmation by the employee. As a result, there had been no constructive dismissal.

■ Redundancy

As mentioned in Chapter 9, redundancy is one of the potentially fair reasons for dismissal. It occurs when an employer requires to dismiss employees for economic reasons, e.g. a downturn in business. The statutory disciplinary and dismissal procedures apply to redundancies – see Chapter 9.

Right to receive a redundancy payment

A redundant employee who has been continuously employed for a period of two years or more has the right to receive a redundancy payment.

KEY STATUTORY PROVISIONS

ERA 1996, s. 135(1)

(1) An employer shall pay a redundancy payment to any employee of his if the employee –

   (a) is dismissed by the employer by reason of redundancy ...

ERA 1996, s. 155

An employee does not have any right to a redundancy payment unless he has been continuously employed for a period of not less than two years ending with the relevant date.

Calculation of statutory redundancy payment

The statutory redundancy payment is calculated as follows:

- a half week's pay for each full year of service where the employee's age during the year is less than 22 years of age;
- one week's pay for each full year of service where the employee's age during the year is 22 years of age or above, but less than 41 years of age; and
- one-and-a-half weeks' pay for each full year of service where the employee's age during the year is 41 years of age or above.

In other words, it is calculated in exactly the same manner as the basic award in the context of unfair dismissal. See Chapter 9 for further details.

REVISION NOTE

Moreover, in problem questions, you should ensure that it is stated that the employee has been continuously employed for at least two years. Otherwise, the employee will not be entitled to a redundancy payment. Furthermore, if an employee rejects suitable alternative employment which is offered by the employer, that employee will forfeit their right to a redundancy payment (ss. 138 and 141 of the ERA 1996).

Definition of 'redundancy'

Redundancy is defined in s. 139(1) of the ERA 1996.

KEY STATUTORY PROVISION

ERA 1996, s. 139(1)

… an employee who is dismissed shall be taken to be dismissed by reason of redundancy if the dismissal is wholly or mainly attributable to –

   (a) the fact that his employer has ceased or intends to cease –

      (i) to carry on the business for the purposes of which the employee was employed by him, or
      (ii) to carry on that business in the place where the employee was so employed, or

   (b) the fact that the requirements of that business–

      (i) for employees to carry out work of a particular kind, or
      (ii) for employees to carry out work of a particular kind in the place where the employee was employed by the employer,

have ceased or diminished or are expected to cease or diminish.

Diminishing requirements – 'work of a particular kind'

Section 139(1)(a)(i) of the ERA 1996 applies where there is a permanent or temporary cessation of the employer's business; in other words, the employer stops trading. Section 139(1)(a)(ii) of the ERA 1996 applies where the employer ceases to carry on its business in a particular place, e.g. the closure of a branch, office or factory. The test of diminishing requirements in s. 139(1)(b) of the ERA 1996 has been the most troublesome of the tests in s. 139(1) of the ERA 1996 for the courts and tribunals to apply. It essentially seeks to cover the situation where the employer has surplus labour, i.e. they require fewer employees for existing work or there is less work for existing employees. Two schools of thought emerged as to how courts and tribunals should ascertain whether the employer's requirements for 'work of a particular kind' had ceased or diminished. The first was the 'contract' test which considered the work which the employee was under a duty to do under the terms of his contract. The second was the 'function' test which instead looked at the work which the employer actually did. Different cases applied different tests, but the matter was settled by the House of Lords in *Murray* v. *Foyle Meats Ltd* (1999).

Murray v. *Foyle Meats Ltd* [1999] IRLR 56

Concerning: 'work of a particular kind', redundancy

Facts

Murray was employed as a meat plant operative in a slaughter hall which was located in the employer's factory. Due to a downturn in business, the employer decided that there was a need to reduce the number of skilled meat plant operatives working in the slaughter hall. After a selection process, Murray was dismissed for redundancy and he claimed that the definition of redundancy in s. 139(1)(b) of the ERA 1996 had not been satisfied.

Legal principle

The House of Lords rejected Murray's appeal. The definition of redundancy in s. 139(1)(b) of the ERA 1996 was simple and asked two questions of fact. The first is whether one or other of various states of economic affairs exists. In this case, this was whether the requirements of the business for employees to carry out work of a particular kind have diminished. The second question is whether the applicant's dismissal was attributable, wholly or mainly, to that state of affairs. Hence, the matter is one of factual causation and is for the tribunal to determine. The House of Lords criticised both the 'contract' and 'function' tests.

FURTHER THINKING

Do you agree with the view of the House of Lords in *Murray* that the 'contract' and 'function' tests miss the point of s. 139(1)(b) of the ERA 1996? If so, what is the purpose of the words 'work of a particular kind' in that subsection?

■ S. Anderman (2000) 'The Interpretation of Protective Employment Statutes and Contracts of Employment' 29 *Industrial Law Journal* 223 at pp. 229–233; and

■ S. Deakin and G. Morris (2005) *Labour Law*, 4th edn, at pp. 535–538. Oxford: Hart Publishing.

'Pools' and selection criteria and procedures

In making the decision as to which members of the workforce will be made redundant, the employer must:

■ choose an appropriate pool of employees for redundancy; and
■ apply fair and proper selection criteria and procedures to the chosen pool.

A fair and proper selection procedure is where employees are graded according to skills, performance, time-keeping, work attendance, abilities and other neutral criteria (e.g. see *British Aerospace plc* v. *Green* (1995)). If the employer has chosen to make ten employees redundant from a pool of clerical staff, then employees in clerical positions with the lowest ten scores would then be made redundant. Provided the process is open and transparent, the benefit of such an approach is that it is based on meritocratic criteria, rather than discriminatory criteria (see Chapters 5 and 6).

Offer of suitable alternative employment

Part of the process of fair and proper selection of employees for redundancy is for the employer to consider suitable alternative employment which might be offered to selected employees. For example, if it is proposed to make a PA redundant, the employer should consider whether a secretarial post might be made available and offered to the PA. A failure on the part of the employer to consider such possible suitable alternatives may result in a finding of unfair dismissal.

Consultation procedures

It is incumbent on an employer to consult with the affected employees and employee representatives or trade unions and to comply with good industrial relations practice.

Good industrial practice

- First, as much warning as possible of the proposed redundancies should be given to employees and trade unions to enable meaningful, fair and genuine consultation to take place.
- Second, the consultation process itself must be fair, meaningful and genuine.
- Third, consultation must take place with the individual employees affected, as well as employee representatives and trade unions.
- Fourth, if there are no selection criteria in a redundancy agreement or collective agreement, the selection criteria should be agreed with the trade unions or employee representatives.
- Fifth, the selection criteria should be transparent, fair and proper and applied properly by the employer.
- Sixth, suitable alternative employment should be considered and, if there is any, duly offered to the selected employees.

REVISION NOTE

In Chapter 9, we referred to the rule in s. 98A(2) of the ERA 1996 that an employer will be able to avoid a finding of unfair dismissal if they can demonstrate that:

I the decision to dismiss fell within the range of reasonable responses; and
I their failure to follow a proper procedure in respect of the dismissal would have made no difference to their decision to dismiss.

The same rule applies in the context of redundancy.

An employer will not be held to have unfairly dismissed an employee if they can demonstrate that:

I the reason for dismissal was genuinely a redundancy in terms of s. 139 of the ERA 1996;
I they applied the minimum statutory dismissal and disciplinary procedures in Part 1 of Sch. 2 to the Employment Act 2002 to the redundancy; and
I their failure to consult and apply fair procedures over and above the statutory dismissal and disciplinary procedures in Part 1 of Sch. 2 to the Employment Act 2002 would have made no difference to their decision to make the employee redundant.

See *Wareing* v. *Stone Cladding International Ltd* (2007).

EXAM TIP

In problem questions, you may be asked whether an individual has been unfairly dismissed for the reason of redundancy. In coming to a view, you should consider whether the facts in the problem state that:

I meaningful, fair and genuine consultation has taken place between the employer and employee, employee representatives and trade union;
I the employer has offered the employee suitable alternative employment; and
I a pool has been chosen and that selection procedures have been agreed and properly applied to that pool.

Rather than a purely factual assessment, some of these issues will require you to make a judgment (e.g. the nature of the selection procedure and whether they are fair and transparent).

Chapter summary
Putting it all together

- [ ] Can you tick all the points from the revision checklist at the beginning of this chapter?
- [ ] Take the **end-of-chapter quiz** on the companion website.
- [ ] Test your knowledge of the cases below with the **revision flashcards** on the website.
- [ ] Attempt the essay question at the beginning of the chapter using the guidelines below.
- [ ] Go to the companion website to try out other questions.

Answer guidelines

See the problem question at the start of this chapter. A diagram illustrating how to structure your answer is available on the website.

Points to remember when answering this question:

- The first major issue is to consider whether the definition of 'redundancy' contained in s. 139(1) of the ERA 1996 has been satisfied in the employee's case.
- You should examine whether the chosen pool for comparison is fair and proper.
- Analyse whether 'past performance' is a fair, proper and neutral selection criterion.
- Explain the effect of the employer's failure to consult with the employee or to offer him suitable alternative employment.
- Has the employer applied the statutory dismissal and disciplinary procedures contained in Part 2 of Sch. 2 to the Employment Act 2002? What is the effect of the employer's failure to do so?

Make your answer stand out
- Consider the implications of *Murray* v. *Foyle Meats Ltd* (1999).

11
Collective labour law

Trade unions

Protection of trade union
membership and activities

Collective
labour
law

Collective bargaining

Statutory recognition procedure

Law of industrial action
and statutory immunities

Revision Checklist

What you need to know:

☐ The law relating to trade unions

☐ The legal protection of trade union membership and activities

☐ Collective bargaining and the statutory recognition of trade unions

☐ The law of industrial conflict.

Introduction:
Understanding collective labour law

Trade union members and trade unions enjoy certain protected rights in relation to industrial disputes

This chapter examines a number of issues which are relevant to collective labour law. The majority of collective labour law is contained in the Trade Union and Labour Relations (Consolidation) Act 1992 and the Employment Relations Act 1999. First, the institution of the trade union is considered, together with the legal definition of a 'trade union' and the meaning of 'independence' of trade unions. Second, the legal protection of trade union membership and activities will be examined. Collective bargaining and the statutory procedures in respect of the recognition of trade unions will be briefly analysed. Finally, the important topic of industrial conflict will be explored.

Essay question advice

Essays require broad general knowledge of the rights and duties of trade unions. You must also understand the statutory recognition procedures which apply to trade unions. An appreciation of some of the issues regarding the liability and statutory immunities of trade unions in tort or delict (in Scotland) may also be required. In tackling essay questions, you should always directly answer the question(s) asked and apply the relevant law.

Problem question advice

Problem questions may involve an examination of a particular trade union's factual circumstances or an individual employee's or employer's factual circumstances. You will be expected to determine whether the trade union, individual or employer has a reasonable prospect of success in pursuing a claim. In tackling problem questions, you should always directly answer the question(s) asked and apply the relevant law to the facts at hand. For example, if the problem question involves an employee who has been persuaded by a trade union to breach their contract of employment with their employer, you should seek to ascertain whether the trade union will have committed the tort of inducing a breach of contract and whether the union enjoys statutory immunity from liability.

Sample question

Could you answer this question? Below is a typical essay question that could arise on this topic. Guidelines on answering the question are included at the end of the chapter, whilst a sample problem question and guidance on tackling it can be found on the companion website.

Essay question

Critically evaluate the statutory immunities from liability conferred on trade unions in the Trade Union and Labour Relations (Consolidation) Act 1992. Is the law satisfactory?

■ Trade unions

Definition of a 'trade union' and legal status

If a body falls within the statutory definition of a 'trade union', certain legal rights and duties will be conferred and imposed upon that body.

> **KEY STATUTORY PROVISION**
>
> **Trade Union and Labour Relations (Consolidation) Act 1992 ('TULRCA 1992'), s. 1**
>
> . . . a 'trade union' means an organisation (whether temporary or permanent) –
>
> (a) which consists wholly or mainly of workers of one or more descriptions and whose principal purposes include the regulation of relations between workers of that description or those descriptions and employers or employers' associations . . .

Legal status of trade unions

Under the common law, a trade union was not treated as a body corporate, i.e. a legal body distinct from its member workers. Instead, it was treated as an unincorporated association. As a result, the trade union had no separate legal personality and so could not be sued in its own name and could not enter into contracts or deeds in its own name. The position is now governed by TULRCA 1992, which ascribes partial, rather than full, corporate status upon a trade union.

KEY STATUTORY PROVISION

TULRCA 1992, s. 10

(1) A trade union is not a body corporate but –

(a) it is capable of making contracts [in its own name];

(b) it is capable of suing and being sued in its own name, whether in proceedings relating to property or founded on contract or tort or any other cause of action; and

(c) proceedings for an offence alleged to have been committed by it or on its behalf may be brought against it in its own name . . .

Section 12(1) of TULRCA 1992 also provides that all property belonging to a trade union shall be vested in trustees in trust for it.

Listing

Section 2 of TULRCA 1992 provides that the Certification Officer of ACAS must maintain a list of trade unions. Where an organisation applies for listing, the Certification Officer will grant a listing provided that he is satisfied that the organisation falls within the definition of a 'trade union' in s. 1 of TULRCA 1992. On the application of an organisation whose name is included in the list, the Certification Officer is under an obligation to issue a certificate that that organisation is listed. The Certification Officer is given power by s. 4 of TULRCA 1992 to remove an organisation from the list if it appears to him that it no longer falls within the definition of a 'trade union'.

Independence

Once an organisation is entered in the list of trade unions, it may apply to the Certification Officer for a certificate of independence. This certificate confirms that the organisation concerned is an 'independent trade union'.

KEY DEFINITION

Independent trade union Section 5 of TULRCA 1992 provides that a trade union is independent if:

(a) it is not under the domination or control of an employer, group of employers or employers' associations; and

(b) it is not liable to interference by an employer (arising out of the provision of financial or material support or by any other means whatsoever) tending towards such control.

Why is 'independent' status important to a trade union?

There are a number of reasons why a trade union will seek a certificate of independence. Some of the reasons are as follows:

▌ employees are treated as automatically unfairly dismissed if they are dismissed for the reason that they are, or propose to become, members of an independent trade union (TULRCA 1992, s. 152);

▌ 'workers' who are members of an independent trade union will enjoy protection from being subjected to a detriment by their employer on the grounds of their union activities (TULRCA 1992, s. 146);

▌ independent trade unions enjoy certain tax reliefs and benefits (Income and Corporation Taxes Act 1988, s. 467); and

▌ only independent trade unions may apply for statutory recognition (para. 6 of Sch. A1 to TULCRA 1992);

FURTHER THINKING

The power and influence of the trade union movement in UK employment relations has decreased significantly over the past forty years. This is evident from the figures of trade union membership which declined from 13.2 million members in 1979 to just under 7.5 million members in 2005/6. Two reasons for this decline are as follows:

▌ Major structural changes in the economy of the UK during the period from 1980 to the present. The UK changed from a manufacturing-based economy to a service-based economy. There was a gradual decline in large manufacturing plants with a large proportion of workers forming part of a union and having one employer. The services sector is more fragmented and the scope for union membership declined.

▌ The anti-union stance of the Conservative Governments between 1979 and 1997. The Conservative Governments introduced incremental reforms which reduced the power of the trade unions over that period. Examples of such ▶

▶ reforms were the restriction of the right of union members to take industrial action, the introduction of ballots for 'closed shops', the disbanding of union recognition machinery and the introduction of rights in favour of union members against trade unions.

Do you believe that there is a continuing role for trade unions in the UK?

■ K. Ewing (2005) 'The Function of Trade Unions' 34 *Industrial Law Journal* 1; and

■ A. Charlwood (2004) 'The New Generation of Trade Union Leaders and Prospects for Union Revitalisation' 42 *British Journal of Industrial Relations* 379.

■ Protection of trade union membership and activities

Union membership: protection from dismissal and detriment

An employee or worker has the right not to be dismissed or subjected to a detriment on grounds related to trade union membership.

KEY STATUTORY PROVISION

TULRCA 1992, s. 152

(1) ... the dismissal of an employee shall be regarded as unfair if the reason for it ... was that the employee –

(a) was, or proposed to become, a member of an independent trade union ... or
was not a member of any trade union, or of a particular trade union ...

The employee's right under s. 152 is enforceable by presenting a complaint to an employment tribunal. If the complaint is successful, the amount of the basic award must not be less than £4,000 (TULRCA 1992, s. 156).

KEY STATUTORY PROVISION

TULRCA 1992, s. 146

(1) A worker has the right not to be subjected to any detriment as an individual by any act, or any deliberate failure to act, by his employer if the act or failure takes place for the sole or main purpose of –

   (a) preventing or deterring him from being or seeking to become a member of an independent trade union, or penalising him for doing so . . . or

   (c) compelling him to be or become a member of any trade union or of a particular trade union . . .

A worker may enforce this right by presenting a complaint to an employment tribunal. If the complaint is successful, the employment tribunal will award compensation which it 'considers just and equitable in all the circumstances' having regard to the infringement complained of and to any loss sustained by the worker which is attributable to the act or failure which infringed his right.

Problem area 'any act, or any deliberate failure to act'?

The words 'any act, or any deliberate failure to act' in s. 146 of TULRCA 1992 cover the conduct and omissions of employers. However, it is not wholly clear whether a threat of adverse consequences by an employer falls within the scope of a detriment. In *Brassington* v. *Cauldon Wholesale Ltd* (1978), Bristow J in the EAT did not decide the issue but, from the tenor of his judgment, one can detect a view that a threat of consequences was not the same thing as a detriment or an 'act'. In *Brassington*, the employer had threatened to cease treading, dismiss the whole of the workforce and resume trading under a new name if the workers joined a union. Meanwhile, the jurisprudence of the European Court of Human Rights, e.g. *Young, James and Webster* v. *UK* (1982) at 417, suggests that a threat of adverse consequences is an illegitimate interference with the worker's Convention rights to join a trade union and thus is contrary to the ECHR.

REVISION NOTE

The implications of a dismissal being held in law to be an 'automatically unfair dismissal' were covered in Chapter 9.

Union activities: protection from dismissal and detriment

An employee or worker has the right not to be dismissed or subjected to a detriment on grounds related to trade union activities.

<table>
<tr><td rowspan="3">KEY STATUTORY PROVISION</td><td>

TULRCA 1992, s. 152

(1) ... the dismissal of an employee shall be regarded as unfair if the reason for it (or, if more than one, the principal reason) was that the employee ...

    (b) had taken part, or proposed to take part, in the activities of an independent trade union at an appropriate time,

    (ba) had made use, or proposed to make use, of trade union services at an appropriate time ...

</td></tr>
</table>

The employee's rights above are also enforceable by presenting a complaint to an employment tribunal. Again, if the complaint is successful, the amount of the basic award must not be less than £4,000 (TULRCA 1992, s. 156).

Problem area 'the activities of an independent trade union'?

It is clear from *Drew* v. *St Edmundsbury BC* (1980) that participation in industrial action, such as strike action, is not covered by s. 152(1)(b) of TULRCA 1992. Moreover, the courts have drawn a distinction between:

1. the situation where a trade union member participates in the kind of activities which his trade union pursues; and
2. the situation where a trade union member participates in the kind of activities which (i) his trade union pursues and (ii) the trade union has authorised that member to do on its behalf.

In the case of 1 above, the courts have held that such activity does not fall within s. 152(1)(b) of TULRCA 1992, whereas in the case of 2 above, the member will indeed enjoy the protection of s. 152(1)(b) – see *Dixon and Shaw* v. *West Ella Developments Ltd* (1978).

TULRCA 1992, s. 146

(1)   A worker has the right not to be subjected to any detriment as an individual by any act, or any deliberate failure to act, by his employer if the act or failure takes place for the sole or main purpose of

. . .

(b) preventing or deterring him from taking part in the activities of an independent trade union at an appropriate time, or penalising him for doing so, [or]

(ba) preventing or deterring him from making use of trade union services at an appropriate time, or penalising him for doing so . . .

Section 146(1)(b) and (ba) of TULRCA 1992 are enforceable in the same fashion as s. 152(1)(b) and (ba) of TULRCA 1992 and compensation is also calculated in the same way as s. 146(1)(a) and (c).

Inducement not to belong to a trade union

In the case of *Wilson and the NUJ* v. *UK* (2002), the European Court of Human Rights held that the UK was in breach of the right to freedom of association under Article 11 of the European Convention on Human Rights by permitting employers to use financial incentives to induce employees to surrender their trade union rights. As a result of this case, the UK Government introduced provisions making such inducements unlawful in ss. 145A–145F of TULRCA 1992.

■Collective bargaining

One of the primary activities of a trade union is to engage in collective bargaining with an employer or an employers' association. The result of successful collective bargaining is a collective agreement.

Definition of 'collective bargaining'

Collective bargaining is defined in s. 178 of the TULRCA 1992.

TULRCA 1992, s. 178

(1) ... 'collective agreement' means any agreement or arrangement made by or on behalf of one or more trade unions and one or more employers or employers' associations and relating to one or more of the matters specified below; and 'collective bargaining' means negotiations relating to or connected with one or more of those matters.

Matters covered by collective bargaining

The matters specified in s. 178(2) of TULRCA 1992 are as follows:

- terms and conditions of employment;
- engagement or non-engagement, or termination or suspension of employment or the duties of employment, of one or more workers;
- allocation of work or the duties of employment between workers or groups of workers;
- disciplinary matters;
- a worker's membership or non-membership of a trade union;
- machinery for negotiation or consultation; and
- facilities for officials of trade unions.

REVISION NOTE

You should be clear that the definition of 'collective bargaining' in s. 178(1) and (2) of TULCRA 1992 is different from the definition of 'collective bargaining' for the purposes of the procedures relating to the statutory recognition of trade unions in Sch. A1 to TULRCA 1992.

There is a presumption that collective agreements are not legally enforceable in a court of law.

TULRCA 1992, s. 179

(1) A collective agreement shall be conclusively presumed not to have been intended by the parties to be a legally enforceable contract unless the agreement –

    (a) is in writing, and

    (b) contains a provision which (however expressed) states that the parties intend that the agreement shall be a legally enforceable contract.

(2) A collective agreement which does satisfy those conditions shall be conclusively presumed to have been intended by the parties to be a legally enforceable contract.

There is a major exception to this rule which we will consider below in the context of the statutory recognition procedure that applies to independent trade unions.

Implications of 'collective bargaining' and collective agreements

Where an independent trade union and employers' association are engaged in collective bargaining, there are certain legal implications, as follows:

■ subject to certain limited exceptions, an employer is under a duty to disclose to union representatives (authorised by the union to carry out collective bargaining), on request, certain information, including:

■ information without which the trade union representative would be to a material extent impeded in carrying on collective bargaining with the employer; and

■ information which it would be in accordance with good industrial relations practice that the employer should disclose to the employer for the purposes of collective bargaining (ss. 181 and 182 of TULRCA 1992); and

■ subject to an exception, any term of a collective agreement which prohibits or restricts the right of workers to engage in strike action or other industrial action is treated as not forming part of any contract between the worker and his employer.

■ Statutory recognition

Application for recognition

Section 70A of, and Sch. A1 to, TULRCA 1992 outline a procedure for the statutory recognition of trade unions. (See Figure 11.1 for a diagram outlining the principal stages in the recognition procedure.) A trade union may make a request for statutory recognition which entitles it to conduct collective bargaining on behalf of a 'bargaining unit'. A 'bargaining unit' is a group of workers. Initially, a request must be made to the

Figure 11.1

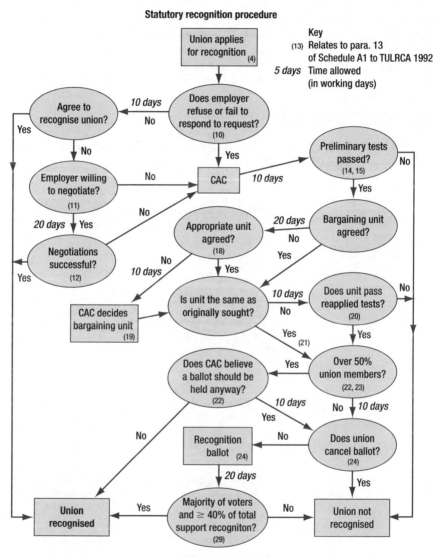

Statutory recognition procedure

Key
(13) Relates to para. 13
of Schedule A1 to TULRCA 1992
5 days Time allowed
(in working days)

Source: Explanatory Notes for the Employment Relations Act 1999, London: HMSO

employer for recognition. If the employer refuses the request and the parties are thus unable to agree recognition voluntarily at this stage, the trade union may apply to the Central Arbitration Committee ('CAC'). The trade union's application will seek a declaration from the CAC awarding it recognition for the purposes of collective bargaining in respect of the specified 'bargaining unit'. The CAC's decision will depend on the degree of support which the union commands within the relevant bargaining unit. The level of support is usually gauged by a secret ballot of all of the workers in the unit. If a majority of the votes cast are in favour of recognition and the number of votes cast represents at least 40% of the total number of workers in the bargaining unit, the CAC will award recognition by declaration. Otherwise, the CAC will issue a declaration that the trade union has no right to recognition.

Collective bargaining

Where a trade union is recognised, it may then conduct 'collective bargaining' with an

Figure 11.2 Establishing the 'Method of collective bargaining'

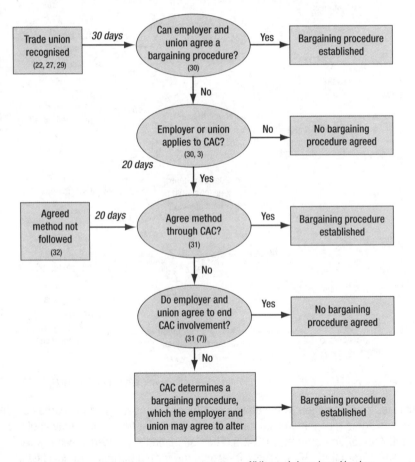

All time periods are in working days

Source: Explanatory Notes for the Employment Relations Act 1999, London: HMSO

employer or employers' association. It is important to stress that 'collective bargaining' has a more limited meaning than 'collective bargaining' for the purposes of s. 178 of TULRCA 1992. Paragraphs 2 and 3 of Sch. A1 to TULRCA 1992 specifically provide that references to collective bargaining are limited to 'negotiations relating to pay, hours and holidays'. This is subject to para. 4, which empowers the union and the employer to add to these matters by agreement.

Method of collective bargaining

Once a trade union has been recognised, its members may negotiate with the employer about the 'method by which they will conduct collective bargaining [with the employer]' (para. 30 of Sch. A1) during the 30-day period commencing the day after the CAC issued the declaration of recognition, or some other longer period mutually agreed by the parties. If the parties are unable to agree the method of collective bargaining within this period, any one of the parties may ask the CAC to specify that method which will bind the parties, subject to variation by mutual agreement in writing. See Figure 11.2 opposite for a diagram which outlines the procedure for agreeing the 'method of collective bargaining'.

The 'method of collective bargaining' imposed by the CAC under Sch. A1 to the TULRCA 1992 'is to have effect as if it were contained in a legally enforceable contract made by the parties'. However, the remedies for breach are limited. Where any of its provisions are breached by one party, the other party is entitled to an order of specific performance only (para. 31(4) and (6) of Sch. A1).

REVISION NOTE

The legal position of such methods of collective bargaining can be contrasted with collective agreements concluded between an employer and trade union generally. You will recall that under s. 179 of TULRCA 1992, collective agreements are presumed not to be legally binding.

The issues covered by the 'method of collective bargaining'

Here, we are concerned with the procedure to be applied by the trade union and the employer for the purposes of conducting negotiations during the period of the statutory recognition arrangements. The 'method' imposes a duty to meet up with each other and discuss issues. It neither imposes a duty on the parties to reach agreement, nor a duty to enter into negotiations with a view to reaching agreement. Issues such as when negotiations are to take place, where they are to take place, which individuals ought to attend, etc., are all covered within the 'method'. A model 'method of collective bargaining' is outlined in the Trade Union Recognition (Method of Collective Bargaining) Order 2000, which is very useful to look at.

Industrial action and statutory immunities

Industrial action Action taken by members of a trade union which imposes restrictions upon employers when collective relations between the employer and the workforce break down.

Examples of industrial action

Examples include the following:

■ strike action (a complete, but temporary, withdrawal of labour);
■ work-to-rule (where the workforce observes the letter of the employer's rule book or procedures, rather than the spirit, thus leading to the disruption of the employer's business); and
■ go-slow action (where the workforce carry out their duties with an appreciable lack of haste, resulting in delays and disruption to the employer's business) and bans on the fulfilment of certain duties.

Industrial action may be lawful or unlawful. Most industrial action in the UK is currently unlawful, i.e. some form of civil liability (e.g. contractual or tortious) will attach to the workers engaged in industrial action or the trade union. This is often the case despite the existence of the statutory immunities.

Liability in tort

Industrial action may lead to civil liability on the part of a trade union. The most common civil liability is tortious liability. This includes:

■ the important tort of inducement to commit a breach of contract;
■ the tort of causing loss to a third party by unlawful means;
■ the tort of intimidation; and
■ the tort of conspiracy.

This revision guide concentrates on the torts of (i) inducement to commit a breach of contract and (ii) causing loss to a third party by unlawful means only.

Inducement to commit a breach of contract

It used to be thought that there were two forms of this tort: the direct form of inducement and the indirect form of inducement. However, the House of Lords unanimously rejected this approach in the case of *OBG Ltd* v. *Allan* (2007). The tort of inducement to commit a breach of contract is satisfied in the following scenario:

▪ Abdul intentionally induces Brian to commit a breach of his contract with Charles without legal justification, which results in loss to Charles. In such a case, Charles will have a right to sue Abdul in tort. The most common example is where a trade union official intentionally persuades an employee member of that trade union to breach their contract of employment with their employer. See Figure 11.3 for a diagrammatical explanation of the tort of inducement to commit a breach of contract. In *OBG Ltd*, the House of Lords clarified that:

▪ Abdul must know that he is inducing a breach of contract and that his intentional actions will have this effect;

▪ Charles must show that Abdul intended to induce Brian to commit a breach of contract. If the breach of Brian's contract with Charles is neither an end in itself nor a means to an end, but merely a foreseeable consequence of the actions of Abdul, then Abdul will not have 'intended' to induce Brian to commit a breach of his contract with Charles; and

▪ this tort imposes secondary or accessory liability on Abdul and requires proof of an actual breach of contract by Brian and thus primary liability on Brian to Charles.

Figure 11.3

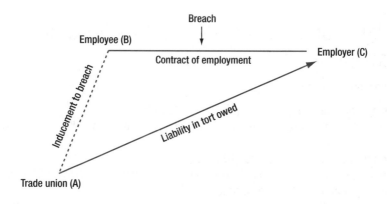

Lumley v. *Gye* [1853] 2 E & B 216

Concerning: inducement to commit a breach of contract

Facts

Miss Wagner had a three-month exclusive contract to sing at Lumley's theatre which was a rival theatre of the theatre owned by Gye. Gye persuaded Miss Wagner to sing at his theatre for a higher fee than she was being paid by Lumley. Gye was aware of Miss Wagner's existing three-month contract. Lumley sued Gye.

Legal principle

The court held that Gye had committed the tort of inducement in directly inducing Wagner to breach her contract with Lumley.

Causing loss to a third party by unlawful means

In the case of *OBG Ltd*, the House of Lords held that a person will cause loss to a claimant by unlawful means where:

▌ that person engages in wrongful interference with the liberty of a third party in which the claimant has an economic interest in a way which is unlawful as against that third party; and
▌ that person has an intention thereby to cause loss to the claimant.

Explanation of 'causing loss to a third party by unlawful means'

Consider the following scenario:

1. A is a trade union, e.g. the Allied Electrician's Union;
2. Bruce is the employee of Comfort plc and is a member of the Allied Electrician's Union;
3. Comfort plc are the employers of Bruce;
4. Comfort plc and Dartmouths plc are in contractual relations whereby Comfort plc supply goods or services to Dartmouths plc;
5. The Allied Electrician's Union wishes to cause economic loss to Dartmouths plc.

If an official of the Allied Electrician's Union persuades Bruce to breach his contract of employment with Comfort plc (and thus induce Bruce to incur a loss by breaching his contract with Comfort plc) with a view to ensuring that Comfort plc are unable to

Figure 11.4

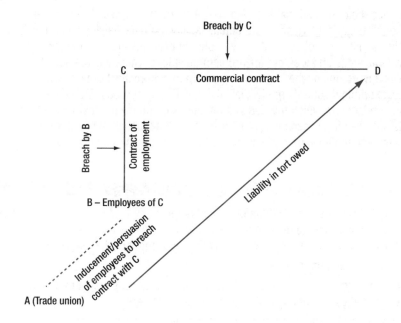

service their commercial contract with Dartmouths plc, thus resulting in loss to Dartmouths plc, then the Allied Electrician's Union will be liable in tort to Dartmouths plc, since they have caused loss to Dartmouths plc by unlawful means. See Figure 11.4.

Statutory immunity

Under statute, trade unions are granted certain immunities from tortious liability.

KEY STATUTORY PROVISION

TULRCA 1992, s. 219

(1) An act done by a person in contemplation or furtherance of a trade dispute is not actionable in tort on the ground only –

(a) that it induces another person to break a contract or interferes or induces another person to interfere with its performance, or

(b) that it consists in his threatening that a contract (whether one to which he is a party or not) will be broken or its performance interfered with, or that he will induce another person to break a contract or interfere with its performance.

EXAM TIP

You must bear in mind that s. 219 of TULRCA 1992 provides immunity from tortious liability only. Hence, contractual liability, criminal liability and other forms of civil liability are not covered. So you should bear this in mind in answering essay questions and look out for problem questions where you are asked to advise a trade union whether they enjoy immunity in respect of facts which indicate criminal conduct or civil liability which is not tortious. Moreover, the torts in relation to which the trade union enjoys immunity are restricted to the torts specified in the section. So other torts such as breach of statutory duty, harassment and libel are not included within the scope of the immunity.

KEY DEFINITION

Section 244 of TULRCA 1992 defines what is meant by **trade dispute** in s. 219 of TULRCA above. A trade dispute means a dispute between workers and their employer which relates wholly or mainly to one or more of the following:

■ terms and conditions of employment;

■ engagement or non-engagement, or termination or suspension of employment or the duties of employment, of one or more workers;

■ allocation of work or the duties of employment between workers;

■ matters of discipline;

■ a worker's membership or non-membership of a trade union;

■ facilities for officials of trade unions; and

■ machinery for negotiation or consultation, including statutory recognition procedures in respect of trade unions.

Exceptions to statutory immunity

There are certain exceptions to the statutory immunity in s. 244 of TULRCA 1992. If any of these exceptions are relevant, the trade union does not enjoy the trade immunity. The exceptions are as follows:

■ The statutory immunity of the trade union is removed and industrial action is not protected unless a majority of union members who are likely to be called out to industrial action have consented to such action pursuant to a ballot carried out in accordance with ss. 226–235 of TULRCA 1992; and

■ If the industrial action is not being taken against the primary employer, the statutory immunity will be removed unless the secondary action is protected secondary action, i.e. lawful picketing falling within s. 224 of TULRCA 1992.

Chapter summary
Putting it all together

☐ Can you tick all the points from the revision checklist at the beginning of this chapter?

☐ Take the **end-of-chapter quiz** on the companion website.

☐ Test your knowledge of the cases below with the **revision flashcards** on the website.

☐ Attempt the essay question at the beginning of the chapter using the guidelines below.

☐ Go to the companion website to try out other questions.

Answer guidelines

See the essay question at the start of this chapter. A diagram illustrating how to structure your answer is available on the website.

Points to remember when answering this question:

■ Give a brief overview of the main torts in the context of industrial action.

■ Explore the scope of the statutory immunities.

■ Examine what is not covered by the statutory immunities.

Make your answer stand out

■ Consider whether the statutory immunities are too restricted.

■ Place the statutory immunities in their historical, political, economic and social contexts by examining the role of Government in restricting their scope in the past 30 years.

And finally, before the exam . . .

By using this revision guide to direct your work, you should now have a good knowledge and understanding of the way in which the various aspects of employment law work in isolation and the many ways in which they are interrelated. What is more, you should have acquired the necessary skills and techniques to demonstrate that knowledge and understanding in the exam, regardless of whether the questions are presented to you in essay or problem form.

TEST YOURSELF

Make sure that before you go into the exam, you:

- [ ] Go through each case in the text and make sure that you know the legal principle of each. You may find it helpful to make a separate list of these cases, write down the name of each and under it leave space for you to write in the legal principle. Facts of cases are only relevant when they explain the principle – never in themselves.

- [ ] Go through each of the statutory provisions which are relevant to a particular topic. Concentrate on the legal principle and remember to use the facts to illustrate the principle. Extract the key words of a statute and learn them.

- [ ] Should remember that employment law exams do require you to be accurate and precise. This means that you must be absolutely clear about the point of a case and/or a statutory provision.

- [ ] Go through each key definition in the guide and understand them.

- [ ] Go to the companion website and revisit the interactive **quizzes** provided for each chapter.

- [ ] Go to the companion website and test your knowledge of cases, statutory provisions and terms with the **revision flashcards**.

Glossary of terms

Key definitions

Fixed-term contract	A contract which endures for a specific period of time and terminates at the end of that period of time.
Implied term of mutual trust and confidence	A term of the contract of employment that each party will not, without reasonable and proper cause, act in such a way as would be calculated or likely to destroy or seriously damage the relationship of trust and confidence existing between it and the other party to the contract.
Independent trade union	A trade union which is not under the domination or control of an employer, group of employers or employers' associations and is not liable to interference by an employer (arising out of the provision of financial or material support or by any other means whatsoever) tending towards such control.
Industrial action	Action taken by members of a trade union which impose restrictions upon employers when collective relations between the employer and the workforce break down.
Repudiatory breach of contract	A breach of a term of a contract which goes to the root of that contract so that on the occurrence of breach the innocent party may be regarded as discharged from further performance of their obligations under the contract.
Trade dispute	A dispute between workers and their employer which relates wholly or mainly to one or more of the following –

- terms and conditions of employment;
- engagement or non-engagement, or termination or suspension of employment or the duties of employment, of one or more workers;
- allocation of work or the duties of employment between workers;
- matters of discipline;

- a worker's membership or non-membership of a trade union;
- facilities for officials of trade unions; and
- machinery for negotiation or consultation, including statutory recognition procedures in respect of trade unions.

Unfair dismissal   The dismissal of an employee which is unfair in terms of Part X of the Employment Rights Act 1996.

Wrongful dismissal   The dismissal of an employee which amounts to a repudiatory breach of contract on the part of the employer.

Other terms

Constructive dismissal   Where an employee terminates the contract under which he is employed (with or without notice) in circumstances in which he is entitled to terminate it without notice by reason of the employer's conduct.

Disability   Where a person has a physical or mental impairment which has a substantial and long-term adverse effect on his ability to carry out normal day-to-day activities.

Employee   An individual who has entered into or works under . . . a contract of employment.

Redundancy   Where an employee's dismissal is wholly or mainly attributable to –

(a) the fact that his employer has ceased or intends to cease –
  (i) to carry on the business for the purposes of which the employee was employed by him, or
  (ii) to carry on that business in the place where the employee was so employed, or
(b) the fact that the requirements of that business –
  (i) for employees to carry out work of a particular kind, or
  (ii) for employees to carry out work of a particular kind in the place where the employee was employed by the employer,

have ceased or diminished or are expected to cease or diminish.

Trade union   An organisation which consists wholly or mainly of workers of one or more descriptions and whose principal purposes include the regulation of relations between workers of that description or those descriptions and employers or employers' associations.

Worker

An individual who has entered into or works under (a) a contract of employment, or (b) any other contract, whereby the individual undertakes to do or perform personally any work or services for another party to the contract whose status is not by virtue of the contract that of a client or customer of any profession or business undertaking carried on by the individual.

Index